Anonymous

The Ladies' indispensable Companion and Housekeepers' Guide

Embracing Rules of Etiquette, Rules for the Formation of good Habits, and a great Variety of medical Recipes

Anonymous

The Ladies' indispensable Companion and Housekeepers' Guide
Embracing Rules of Etiquette, Rules for the Formation of good Habits, and a great Variety of medical Recipes

ISBN/EAN: 9783337184117

Printed in Europe, USA, Canada, Australia, Japan

Cover: Foto ©Lupo / pixelio.de

More available books at **www.hansebooks.com**

THE LADIES INDISPENSABLE COMPANION

AND

HOUSEKEEPERS' GUIDE:

EMBRACING

RULES OF ETIQUETTE; RULES FOR THE FORMATION OF GOOD HABITS;

AND A GREAT

VARIETY OF MEDICAL RECIPES.

TO WHICH IS ADDED ONE OF THE

Best Systems of Cookery

EVER PUBLISHED.

THE MAJORITY OF THE RECIPES ARE NEW AND OUGHT TO BE POSSESSED BY EVERY ONE.

New-York:
H. DAYTON, 36 HOWARD STREET;
INDIANAPOLIS, IND.: ASHER & CO.
1860.

CONTENTS.

A.

	Page.
Ague	29
Air	10
Asiatic Cholera	23
Asthma, Cure of	14

B.

Bilious Cholic	36
Bilious Complaints	36
Bite of Poisonous Creatures	33
Bleeding at the Lungs	34
" " Stomach	47
" from the Nose	16
Bloody Urine	34
Boils	29
Bowel Complaints in Children	42
Burn or Scald	25
Burns	50

C.

Cancer	42
Callus	30
Catarrh	30
Certain Cure for a Cold	24
Chilblain	32
Cholera, Morbus	16
Consumption, No. 1.	15
Consumptive Cough	46
Continued Fever	19

	Page
Convulsion Fits	44
Corns	32
Costiveness in Children	9
Coughs and Colds do.	9
Cough	48
Cough, Recipe for	24
Courses, painful	33
Cow-pox	22
Cramp in the Stomach	30
Croup, No. 1.	10
Croup, No. 2.	38
Cutting Teeth	35

D.

Deafness	34
Delirium Tremens	26
Diabetes	42
Diarrhœa	15
Distress after Eating	45
Dropsy	35
Dropsy of the Head	12
Drowning, recovery from	26
Dysentery	15
Dyspepsia	37

E.

Earache, No. 1.	30
Earache, No. 2.	44
Elecampane for a Cough	25
Epeleptic Fits	44
Eyes, Inflammation of	20

CONTENTS.

	Page.
Eyes, Sore and Weak	37
Eyes, Weaping	50

F.

	Page.
Falling of the Bowels in Children	29
Felon in the Eye	27
Felon on the Hand	38
Female Obstructions	14
Fever and Ague	27
Fever Sore	28
Fits or Convulsions in Children	11
Flaxseed Tea	25
Flour Albus	38
Food for Children	11
Food for Infants brought up by hand	10
Frost Bite	50

G.

	Page.
Gleets	47
Good Remedy for Fits	48
Gout	37
Gravel or Stone, No. 1	39
Gravel or Stone, No. 2	43

H.

	Page.
Headache, Sick	28
Hiccough	29
Hoarseness	47
Humors. No. 1.	36
Humors. No. 2.	47
Hysterics	50

I

	Page.
Inflammatory Fever	16
Itch	33

J.

	Page.
Jaundice	32
Joints, Stiffened	48

K.

	Page.
Keeping Children clean	11
King's Evil	48

L.

	Page.
Lame Feet	50
Liver Complaint, No. 1	40
Locked Jaw	52

M.

	Page.
Measles	20
Medicine for Children	9
Menstrual Discharges	31
Mortification	40
Mumps	27

N.

	Page.
Nervous Affections	34
Nipples Sore	45
Numb Palsy	34

O.

	Page.
Old and Inveterate Sores	43
Old Sores to Cure	49

P.

	Page.
Pains	30
Painter's Cholic	43
Palpatation of the Heart	31
Pectoral Syrup for Coughs	25
Piles	43
Piles, Bleeding	45
Phthisic	46

CONTENTS.

	Page.
Pimples	49
Poisons, taking, Tartar Emetic	46
Poisons, Saltpetre	46
" Laudanum	46
" Lunar Caustic.	46
" Corros. Sublimate	47
Polypus	37

R.

Raising Blood	33
Rattlesnake Bites.	24
Rattles in Children	28
Recipes for Rheumatism	19
Remedy for Dropsy in the Head	13
Rheumatic Plaster	23
Rickets, symptoms of	11
Rickets, Remedy for	12
Ring Worm.	41
Rupture	38

S.

Salt Rheum.	35
Scarlet Fever	20
Scrofula, Humor	35
Scrofula	13
Scrofula, Remedy for	13
Scurvy	28
Sleep, to Procure it	48
Smallpox	21
Sore Throat, Common.	44
Sore Throat, Putrid	19
Sore Legs	33
Sore Lips	44
Spine Complaints	49
Sprains	28
St. Anthony's Fire	46

	Page.
Stomach Sickness	34
Strengthening Plaster	38
Strained Stomach	38
St. Vitus' dance	39
Sweat	47
Swellings, to reduce them	29
Swellings, No. 2	26

T.

Tape Worm	40
Teething and Diarrhœa in Children	10
Tic Doloreaux	27
Toothache, No. 1	23
" No. 2	41
" No. 3	50
Treatment of Children	9
Typhus Fever	17

U.

Ulcer	45
Ulcer, Inward	45
Universal Cure all	51
Urinary Discharges, too free	30
Urinary Obstructions	30

V.

Varioloid	21
Volatile Liniment	27
Vomiting prevented	46
Warts, No. 1	24
Warts, No. 2	45
Weak Eyes	49
Weak Limbs	29
Weak Stomach	41
Wen	40
White mixture for a Cough, No. 1	25
" No. 2	25
Whites	49

CONTENTS.

	Page.
White Swelling	35
Whooping Cough, No. 1	14
Whooping Couge, No. 2	40
Windy Stomach	47
Worms	40

Medical Properties of Plants.

A.

	Page.
Aloes	53
Arrow Head	53
Avens or Chocolate Root	53

B.

Black Alder Bark	54
Blackberry Root	54
Black Snake Root	54
Blood Root	54
Blue Flag Root	55
Butter or Oil Nut	54
Butter Cup or Crow's foot	55

C.

Camomile	55
Canada Snake Root	56
Caraway	55
Carrots	55
Catnip	56
Checkerberry	56
Comfrey	56
Currants	56

D.

Dandelion	56
Dragon's Claw or Fever-root	57
Dwarf Elderberries	57

E.

	Page.
Elder blows, bark and berries	57
Elecampane	57

F.

Fever-root	58
Fir Balsam	58
Foxglove	58

G.

Garlic	59
Gentian	59
Ginger	58
Golden Thread	58
Gum Arabic	59

H.

Hemlock bark	60
Hoarhound	60
Hops	60
Horse Radish	59
Hyssop	59

I.

Iceland Moss	60
Indian Hemp	60

J.

Juniper bush	62

K.

Knot Grass	61

L.

Lady's Slipper	62

CONTENTS.

	Page.		Page.
Liquorice	62	**R.**	
Liverwort	63		
Lobelia	61	Red Cedar	66

M.   **S.**

Mosses	63	Sassafras	65
Motherwort	63	Smart-weed	65
Mouse Ear	63	Spikenard	66
Mullen	63	Sumach	65
Mustard (garden)	64		

P.   **T.**

Thorn-apple - 66

Plantain	64
Pennyroyal	64
Poplar Bark (root)	64
Prickly Ash	64

MEDICAL PREPARATIONS.

Q.

Elixir	66
Vegetable Powder	66

Quassia - 65

THE LADIES' COMPANION,

AND

FAMILY PHYSICIAN.

TREATMENT OF CHILDREN.

It is of the greatest importance that mothers should understand the management of their offspring. The newly-born child should be kept warm and not exposed to sudden changes of temperature or currents of air. It should not be handled but kept as quiet as possible.

Medicines.

Never give medicine to a very young child. Many have thus lost darling children. It will, if not murdered, be permanently injured. It cries often on account of tight clothes or the pricking of pins. If medicine must be given at all, give it to the nurse.

Coughs and Colds.

To prevent these, let children wear flannel undergarments. Sometimes it may be necessary to induce redness on the chest by a mustard plaster placed between two cloths.

Costiveness.

Administer a little barley-water and it will remove it

Teething and Diarrhœa.

When the teeth begin to appear, an irritation is produced, and a diarrhœa often sets in to carry it off, in order to keep it from the brain. Let it run while the discharges have the natural color; when the color of the discharges change, lance the gums of the child if there is much heat about them. If the head becomes unusually warm, keep cloths around it wet with moderately cold water. If the diarrhœa still continues, a little arrow-root gruel will generally check it; sometimes it will be necessary to add a tea-spoonful of powdered chalk to a cup-full of the gruel.

Croup.

Take a dose of lobelia sufficient to act as an emetic, and an hour after it has operated, administer a dose of syrup made in the following manner, viz.: a quarter pound elecampane roots, same quantity boneset leaves and blossoms, and a pint of honey. Pulverise the roots and leaves well, put them into an earthen vessel containing the honey, and place the compound in a hot oven for about an hour, or until reduced to half the first quanty. A tea-spoonful administered three times a day is a dose.

Air.

Let children have pure air, but keep the room warm.

If the mother is much diseased, rather than run much risk, bring the child up by hand.

Food for Infants brought up by Hand.

Take two parts of good cow's milk to one part of water, and sweeten it a little with loaf sugar. Warm it so as to be of the temperature of milk just taken from the cow.

Fits or Convulsions.

Put them into warm baths. Do not have the water too hot as their skin is tender. Take them out after a little time and put strong mustard-plasters on the soles of their feet, and ice-water on the head. If the fit has been caused by something eaten, give an emetic of five grains of Ipecac., if the child is under the age of two years and a half, and eight grains if over that age. Vomiting will throw all the medicine up so that the child will not be injured. If the fit arises from other causes, half a table-spoonful of Epsom-salts, dissolved in a fourth of a glass of water for a child two years of age.

Keep the Child Clean.

Wash it every morning in warm water, and never, as some have done, plunge it in cold water.

Food.

It should receive its food at regular hours, three or four times a day, and it should not be permitted to take so much as to cause vomiting. The stomach of a new-born infant is very small, not larger than a common sized thimble, so that there is great danger of giving it too much food.

Rickets.

Symptoms. — Breast-bone protruded, large head, very prominent forehead ; large, puffed-up belly ; joints large ; system weak and movements slow. Finally a slow fever, cough, and troubled breathing ensue, and death often closes the scene.

Remedy for Rickets.—Rectify the general health, give simple, nourishing diet. In case of poor appetite, give five grains of Ipecac. as an emetic. If costive give a little Rhubarb. Wear flannel and be in the open air, and apply warm fermentations to the belly. After each meal half a drop of Lugol's solution of Iodine may be given three times a day.

Rickets.—*By another Physician.*

Easily known by the large head and protruded breast bone, the forehead stares out prominently; the ribs are flattened; the belly is very large and puffed out; the muscles soft: the joints very large in proportion to what they should be : the whole system is very weak and every movement is made slowly and with difficulty.

As the disease progresses the belly becomes harder and the bowels very loose; a slow fever succeeds with cough and trouble in breathing, until death finally comes to the relief of the sufferer.

It generally attacks children between the ages of nine months and two years. The object of the treatment is to build up the general health. Look well to the child's diet, let it be simple and nourishing : if the appetite is poor, an emetic of five grains of Ipecac. will be useful; if the bowels are too much bound, gentle doses of rhubarb is the best medicine to open them, as it strengthens at the same time. As the bones and the spine of the back are often distorted, means must be used to give support wherever needed. The child should wear flannel, and be much out in the open air. Warm fomentations applied to the belly will often be attended with considerable benefit. I have given in this disease Lugol's solution of Iodine, half a drop three times a day, with marked success: it must be given immediately after each meal.

Dropsy of the Head.

Symptoms of the disease in a child.—He rolls his head often from side to side; has pain; a stupid look; perhaps sickness at the stomach and vomiting; slow pulse; and frequent convulsions. When children are thirteen years of age, they are rarely attacked with it. It is often induced by falls or blows, and it is almost impossible to cure it.

Remedy for Dropsy of the Head.—Take considerable blood from the temples by leeches, give powerful cathartics, shave the head and apply to it ice in bladders, apply mustard to the feet and inside of the thighs and make the diet light, mostly of barley. This is about all that can be done.

Scrofula.

Symptoms.—A smooth fine skin, almost transparent fair hair, rosy cheeks, joints large, upper lip prominent, and eyes often very bright. Little round or egg-shaped tumors under the skin appear on the sides of the neck, in winter and spring. The tumors sometimes continue through life without any apparent alteration; but finally they become larger, of a purple or livid color, form matter and break, not at one point, but into many little holes from which a thickish watery discharge oozes, in which is mixed little substances resembling milk curds. Open sores remain for some time afterwards, eating their way in various directions: sometimes after continuing in this way for years, all dry up and disappear. In other cases, blindness results, and deafness ensues: the joints also enlarge, and produce white swelling.

Remedy for Scrofula.

The great object in the treatment is to improve the general health; for this purpose, the means recommended in Rickets may be advantageously used; but the main reliance in every case must be placed in the preparations of Iodine, particularly Lugol's solution Treat scrofulous sores like other sores.

Whooping Cough.

Mix a quarter pound ground elecampane root in half pint strained honey and half pint of water. Put them in a glazed earthen pot, and place it in a stone oven with half the heat required to bake bread. Let it bake until about the consistency of strained honey and take it out. Administer in doses of a tea-spoonful before each meal, to a child; if an adult, double the dose. The diet should be of a warming nature, light and nourishing, so as to create no unnecessary exertion on the part of the patient.

Asthma.

A compound of one oz. each, spikenard root, sweet flag root, elecampane root, and common chalk, beaten or ground very fine, with the addition of a half pound strained honey, is the Indian remedy for this disease, and will generally, if care be used, effect a cure in a short time; the dose being a tea-spoonful after each meal and just before going to bed. When it is inconvenient to procure the above articles, for temporary relief, an application of a mustard plaster to the chest, and immersion of the feet in hot water, with a handful of mustard thrown in, will be found useful, and if the patient is conscientiously opposed to smoking, procure a quantity of the dried leaves of the stramonia plant, and a pipe, and let him make a free use of it, as it has a great tendency to remove mucus from the throat. A warm room, and plenty of covering at night, are absolutely necessary in treatment for this disease.

Female Obstructions.

Take one table-spoonful tincture of guaiacum in half a cup of milk, at the full of the moon; or,

Take a strong tea made of Seneca snakeroot, as much as the stomach will bear; or,

Take of borax, saffron, myrrh, each ten grains; salt of amber, four grains; this may be taken at one dose.

Consumption.

Dissolve chloride of lime in soft water, add a little vinegar, and snuff it up the nose three or four times a day; or,

Take one pound of hops to two quarts of water; reduce by boiling to one quart; add of molasses and gin each one gill; take one table-spoonful morning, noon, and night. And at ten o'clock, A. M., and four o'clock, P. M., a pill may be taken, made as follows: extract of cicuta, one ounce; oxide of zinc, half an ounce; if this does not afford relief, nothing will; or,

Take every morning, half a pint of new milk and the juice of hoarhound, mixed; or,

Take sumach leaves, make into a tea, and drink freely; or,

Of the tincture of gum guaiacum, take a table-spoonful at night; and two or three spoonfuls during the day.

Dysentery.

Take of cherry-rum and brandy, each half a pint, half a pound of loaf sugar, two ounces of essence of peppermint. Dose, one spoonful two or three times a day; or,

Make a strong tincture of rhubarb and of opium, and a strong solution of white vitriol; mix together equal parts. Dose, twenty drops; in one hour, ten drops; and then five—this is a dose for children; or,

Take of laudanum, tincture of camphor, tincture of guaiacum, tincture gum kino, each one drachm. Dose, tea-spoonful three times a day.

Diarrhœa.

Take of opium, gum guaiacum, camphor, each one part; gum kino and ipecac. each half a part; mix into common sized pills. Dose, from one to four per day; or,

Take prepared chalk two drachms, loaf sugar one drachm, add one ounce of gum Arabic, eight ounces of water, oil of lavender one drachm, laudanum thirty drops. Shake it well when you use it. Dose, one table-spoonful every hour; oftner if necessary.

Cholera Morbus.

Take two ounces of the leaves of the Bene plant, which can be procured at almost at any drug store; dissolve in half a pint cold water, an hour, and take it in doses of two table-spoonfuls, hourly, until relief is experienced, which will almost invariably be the case, as I have never yet known it to fail in any case which has come under my observation. This plant is considered by the natives of the West Indies, where it grows indigenously, as invaluable in this distressing disease.

Bleeding from the Nose.

The idea of this proceeding from the ruptured blood-vessel is ridiculous; it is a means taken by nature of thoroughly depleting a part so as to secure disease. It was no doubt in consequence of observing these sanguineous depletions of nature, that the idea originated of doing it artificially, and thence the introduction of blood-letting in all its various forms of abstraction.

If bleeding from the nose proceeds to an alarming extent, it can generally be stopped by plugging up the nostrils with cotton, wet in cold alum water. Sometimes all local means prove ineffectual, nature must have blood escape, and the only method of preventing a flow from the nostrils will be by making one from the arm.

The water-cure method of getting rid of coughs and colds is to wrap the body up in a wet sheet, until perspiration is induced, drinking all the time plenty of cold water.

Inflammatory Fever.

This fever comes on by a sense of weakness and inactivity, succeeded by dizziness, shiverings, and pains extending over the whole body, particularly the chest and back; these symptoms are shortly followed by redness of the face and eyes, great restlessness, intense heat, unquenchable thirst, oppressed breathing and nausea. The skin is dry and parched; the tongue of a scarlet color at the sides, furred with white in the centre; the urine red and scanty; bowels costive; there is a quickness and hardness in the pulse which is not affected by pressure. If allowed to proceed, these symptoms become rapidly more intense, stupor and delirium succeed, with violent raving. At the end of fourteen days it terminates in a crisis, either by sweating, looseness of bowels, bleeding from the nose, or a deposit in the urine, which produces a copious sediment: the pulse softens gradually toward the fourteenth day.

The danger is generally proportioned to the violence of the delirium; if there is picking at the bed-clothes, starting of the tendons, involuntary passages by stool and urine, it will certainly terminate fatally.

Bleeding from the arm, with the patient in an upright position, to fainting, will often cut short the disease at once. The bowels should be well purged with salts and senna, or jalap and cream of tartar. (ten grains of jalap and thirty of cream of tartar to the dose). Perspiration should be induced by giving three grains of James' powder and two of nitre, every two hours until it is freely established—then giving it at longer intervals. The patient must be put in a cool room, where it is rather dark and perfectly quiet. The diet should mainly consist of barley-water, with a very little nitre dissolved in it to quench the thirst; for this latter purpose, also, pieces of ice may be taken in the mouth and allowed to melt. The clothing should be of the lightest kind. It is proper to repeat the bleeding the second day, if there is no remission of symptoms.

Sometimes a particular organ, as the brain or lungs, becomes affected; in such cases, besides the general treatment, use the same means as if inflammation of such organ were alone the matter.

Typhus Fever.

This first comes on with great weakness, low spirits,

excessive weariness and general soreness, with pains in the head, back, and extremities, succeeded by shiverings; the eyes appear full, heavy, yellowish, and often a little inflamed, the arteries of the temple throb violently, the tongue is dry and parched, breathing laborious, interrupted with deep sighing; the breath is hot and offensive, urine pale, bowels costive; the pulse quick, small, hard and unequal. Sometimes a great heat, load, and pain is felt in the pit of the stomach, followed by profuse bilious vomiting. As the disease advances, the pulse becomes more frequent, the fever, higher, breathing difficult, with anxiety, sighing and moaning; the thirst increases; the inside of the mouth becomes covered with a sticky brownish or black fur—speaking becomes difficult, and then not understood; and muttering and delirium ensue, Finally, as it proceeds, all the symptoms become worse; there is bleeding from the gums and various parts of the body; livid spots appear on the surface, and hiccup ushers in death. In warm climates, this fever seldom continues above a week; but in colder ones it lasts three or four.

An emetic of twenty grains of Ipecac, and one of tartar emetic, may be at once administered: let the bowels then be emptied by a large dose of castor oil: then give small doses of Ipecac and Squills to promote perspiration. In cases where the skin keeps hot and dry, sponge it from head to foot with cold water in which a little vinegar is mixed; but where the patient is very low, and the skin cold, the tepid bath will better assist the sweating. A very light vegetable diet should be pursued, except where there is positive sinking, and then it must be more nutritious, wine is allowed in such cases, given according to urgency: wine whey is also useful.

Virginia Snakeroot or Camomile infusions are given to strengthen the system; also a few drops of oil o. vitriol in every pitcher of water that is drunk. Ripe fruits, such as have a sour taste, are highly recommended. Keeping the bowels open by gentle medicines or injections, and being careful that extreme cleanliness and ventilation is attended to, will complete the cure If spots appear in the mouth, gargles of goldthread and honey, with a little alum, are useful to remove them.

If there is much mental anxiety or tremors, mustard plasters should be applied to the feet, or these bathed as high as the knees in mustard and hot water ; and a tea-spoonful of ether or ten grains of Dover's powder taken to induce rest.

I have heard of typhus fever in which all hope was gone, and yet the patients recovered by yeast given by the wine-glassful every three hours.

Continued Fever,

Is so called, when it begins in the same manner as the inflammatory fever, but ends in typhus, seeming to be a blending of both. As it assumes the appearance of one or the other, it must be treated accordingly.

Yellow Fever and *Ship Fever* are names for varieties of Typhus.

Receipe for Rheumatism.

Take 4 ounces Castile soap ; 2 ounces Camphor; half an ounce of Oil Rosemary ; 3 pints Alcohol.

Soak the soap three days in the Alcohol and then add the other ingredients.

Another.

Equal quantities horse raddish roots, elecampane roots, Prince's pine leaves, prickly ash bark, bittersweet root bark, wild cherry bark, and mustard seed, and a pint of tar water, boiled in two quarts of brandy. Drink a wine glass before each meal, and bathe the part affected with salt and rum, before a large fire.

Receipe for Putrid Sore Throat.

Mix one gill of strong apple vinegar, one table-spoonful of common salt, one table-spoonful of drained honey and a half pod of red pepper together, boil them to a proper consistency, then pour it into half pint of strong sage tea, take a tea-spoonful occasionally and it will be found an infallible cure.

Measles.

SYMPTOMS.—Chilliness, shivering, pain in the head, fever, sickness, and sometimes vomiting; dry cough, heaviness of the eyes, with swelling, inflammation, and discharge of watery humor from them, and also from the nostrils. The third or fourth day, an eruption like fleabites appears in the face, neck, and breast, and soon after in the body and limbs. The fever and other symptoms do not, as in the small pox, &c., abate on the appearance of the eruption, which continues about three days, then dries away, the skin peeling off; but the other symptoms remain, and even increase, especially the cough, which is also attended in general with difficulty of breathing, and oppression of the chest.

TREATMENT.—Cooling and aperient febrifuges; gentle diaphoretics; bleeding, if of a plethoric habit and the lungs weak; pectorals with expectorants for the cough; opiates occasionally at night; blisters, if the cough be obstinate; and bathing the feet in warm water. The tincture of digitalis, combined with nitre and syrup of poppies, to abate the cough, may be given instead of opium, according to circumstances.

Scarlet Fever. (Simple.)

SYMPTOMS.—The usual precursory symptoms of a fever, viz., shivering, heal, &c. Then an efflorescence of scarlet color appears all over the skin, but does not rise above the surface; with heat, dryness, and itching. In three or four days it disappears, and the cuticle comes off in branny scales.

TREATMENT.—Cooling saline febrifuges, with mild aperients and diaphoretics, if necessary.

Small Pox.

SYMPTOMS.—The fever preceding the eruption is attended by pains in the loins and back, much drowsiness, and the occurrence of epileptic fits prior to its appearance, is by no means uncommon. The first appearance of the eruption is like flea-bites, which usually come out first on the face, neck, and breast, and successively extend over the body. About the fifth or sixth day, a small vesicle, with a depression in the centre, and containing a nearly colorless fluid, is observable on the top of each pimple; on the eleventh day the matter in the pustule has changed to an opaque yellow, and the hands and feet begin to swell. In the confluent species, the fever is more violent, the eruptions break out in a more hurried and irregular manner, assuming an erythematic character, run into each other, and do not suppurate kindly. Typhoid symptoms appear, and petechiæ appear on the skin, and blood is discharged too by urine and stool.

TREATMENT.—In the distinct small-pox, merely enjoining a cool regimen and saline febrifuges, if the fever run high, with gentle laxatives; and, if there be much restlessness, syrup of poppy. In the confluent kind the treatment is rather that demanded in the putrid fever. If there be a tendancy to sinking, the sub-carbonate of ammonia will be of service; and if the brain be affected, local means may be used. If convulsions appear, give opium with the use of the tepid bath. To prevent the eyes being injured, cold lotions may be applied; and, if necessary, blisters behind the ears.

Varioloid, or Modified Smallpox.

This disease occcurs in consequence of exposure to smallpox contagion of a constitution previously acted upon by the cowpox. Persons may take the smallpox twice, and such cases I have seen personally, but they can never take it if properly vaccinated—the only disease with which they can then be affected is the va_rioloid.

The varioloid, in the majority of cases, is preceded by a slight fever, though instances occur in which it is as violent as in severe smallpox: the eruption then appears in successive clusters, coming-out in no certain period, in different cases of disease, but varying from the fever, so that the patient often gets up when the pustules come out. A red flush or rash, resembling measles, not unfrequently comes out before the pimples; these much resemble the milder cases of chicken-pock, and many times the small, firm red, raised spots are changed to little watery bladders, in the course of the first or second day; many times, however, they dry off at once. Sometimes the little bladders become filled with a fluid resembling matter, and are a little flattened in the centre, but change by the third or fourth day into thin dark scabs, which separate, and drop off by the seventh day. The vesicles rarely or never pit the skin, though warty substances have remained after them.

This disease, of course, requires only a light diet, free access of air, and open bowels, to get well of itself; if any other symptoms arise, directions for the treatment may be found under the head of smallpox.

Cowpox—Vaccination.

A clearly defined circular space, not very large, with appearances of lines running from the centre to the edges, and full of punctures—will mark the genuine cowpox sore. The seventh day is the best time for taking out the matter: slightly cut the edge of the pustule and press it gently out, then rolling the quills in it and allowing the lymph to dry on them.

In order to vaccinate, cut a piece of one of the quills to a sharp point, and having first pushed the lancet or blade of a penknife a little way under the skin, insert the quill in the incision, and allow it to remain there some five or ten minutes, that will be sufficient.

If inflammation of the arm follows, treat it on the ordinary plan.

Toothache.

Equal proportions of Cajeput Oil and Olive Oil, dropped on cotton and placed in the cavity of the tooth, or even round the tooth, generally gives relief.

Rheumatic Plaster.

Half a pound of Rosin, and half a pound of Sulphur, melt them by a slow fire, then add one ounce of Cayenne and half an ounce of Camphor-gum; stir well till it is mixed, and temper it with Neats' foot oil.

Asiatic Cholera.

Take Spirits of Camphor, 3 drachms; Spirits of Turpentine, 3 drachms; Laudanum, 3 drachms; Oil of Peppermint, 50 drops; mix all together and shake it well before using it. Dose, one tea-spoonful in some brandy and sugar. This may be taken every half hour for four or five times in succession, till the patient is relieved; but besides this, rubbing with camphor spirits, and flax-seed tea for drink, must be used, and dry heat in the room and around the body to get him in a perspiration; by commencing in this manner, and then calling in a doctor as soon as possible, every one will be safe that may be attacked. The writer has been an eye witness to many cases affected in this way. He says the cases commence by sudden cramps, with a cold sensation. Others with a severe dysentery and vomiting. Others with severe griping or colics. The above is a certain cure in all these cases.

Half a pint best French Brandy; 12 drops Oil Peppermint; 24 drops Laudanum; a table-spoonful every ten minutes till recovered.

Or, equal parts of Laudanum and Spirits Camphor.

Or, equal parts of Laudanum, Spirits Camphor, and strong essence of Peppermint.

To Cure Rattle-Snake Bites.

Chew and swallow, or drink, dissolved in water alum, the size of a hickory nut.

Put thoroughwort leaves pounded on and keep wetting them with water. If the person is very sick, black or purple, let him drink a little of the juice. Renew the application after 2 hours.

Warts.

These troublesome and often painful excrescences, covering the hands sometimes to the number of a hundred or two, may be destroyed by a simple, safe and certain application. Dissolve as much common washing soda as the water will take up, then wash the hands or warts with this for a minute or two, and allow them to dry without being wiped. This repeated for two or three days, will gradually destroy the most irritable wart.

Recipe for a Cough.

Take equal quantities of Hoarhound and Liquorice Root, make a strong decoction, and to three-fourths of a pint of this liquor, add the following ingredients:—

A drachm and a half of dried Squills, half drachm of pure Opium; half drachm of Benzoin; half drachm of Camphor; half drachm of Oil of Aniseed, and two ounces of Honey, simmer it in an earthen vessel, until reduced to a half pint, and when strained and cold, add half a pint of good Old Rum. Take a tea-spoonful any time the cough is troublesome.

Certain Cure for a Cold.

Take three cents' worth of liquorice, three of rock candy, three of gum-arabic, and put them into a quart of water; simmer them till thoroughly dissolved, then add three cents' worth of paragoric, and a like quantity of antimonial wine.

Cough Elecampane.

Make a syrup by slicing the fresh root, covering them with sugar, and baking them for an hour or two.

Flax-Seed Tea.

For severe colds, attended with feverish symptoms, the following is an excellent remedy: Hot flax-seed tea, with lemon-juice and sugar, and fifteen drops of Wine of Ipecac., taken when getting into a warm bed. A few spoonfuls should be taken whenever there is an inclination to cough. Some add two or three spoonfuls of White Mixture or one tea-spoonful of Paregoric, to a tumbler full.

Pectoral Syrup for Coughs.

Gum-arabic, two ounces; Syrup of Tolu, 1 ounce; Paregoric, 2 drachms; Wine of Ipecac., half an ounce.

The White Mixture No. 2 for the Same.

Five ounces of Lac Ammoniac; Syrup of Tolu, one ounce; Wine of Ipecac., half an ounce; Paregoric, half an ounce.

White Mixture No. 1, For a Cough.

Gum Ammoniac, one-fourth of an ounce rubbed in water, two ounces; add Paregoric, half an ounce; Antimonial Wine, half an ounce; Syr Bals. Tolu, one ounce. Dose, a table-spoonful once, twice, or thrice a day, as occasion require. Sweeten with loaf-augar.

Burn or Scald.

Spread a plaster of Turner's cerate, and apply it to the wound twice a day; or,

Burn the inside sole of an old shoe to ashes and sprinkle the ashes on the affected parts

FAMILY PHYSICIAN.

To take down Swelling.

White beans merely stewed soft, and put in thin muslin bags. A poultice of the roots of Yellow Water Lily is very powerful in drawing tumors to a head.

For Inflamed Eyes

Stir the whites of two eggs briskly with a lump of alum till they coagulate, placed on the closed lid at night.

Recovery from Drowning.

There have been many extraordinary recoveries where the body has lain for hours under water; but in general there is not much hope after an immersion of ten minutes.

After the body is taken out of the water, use it as gently as possible; let no violence of any kind, such as rolling on a barrel, be permitted: of course, incline the head at first, that the water may run off; place the body in a warm bed and cover with a warm blanket; hot bricks, or bottles of water should be placed to the feet and hands; and while one or two persons are rubbing assiduously the body with the palms of the hands, let another try to fill the lungs with air: to do this, close the nostrils of the subject, and fittting your mouth to his, blow steadily and forcibly until the chest is full of air then press the bowels upwards, that it may be ejected; this should be repeated a number of times until some signs of life are shown. An injection, in which there is spirits of terpentine, may be thrown up. Gentle stimulants may be given on recovery.

Delirium Tremens.

When the fever is violent, and there is considerable determination to the head, it is well to lower the general tone of the system, by giving nauseating doses of ipecac. as 2 grains every hour, or a tea-spoonful of antimonial wine every hour and a half, until sickness at the stomach is felt. Then give from a half to a whole tea-spoonful of laudanum, and induce sleep.

Volatile Liniment.

Two-thirds sweet-oil, and one-third hartshorn, shaken well and corked very tight. Rubbed on stiff necks, rhumatic limbs, and to prevent sore-throat.

Tic Doloreux.

This dreadful disease is treated by strengthening the general system, and the use of tonic medicines, as quinine and salacine.

Mesmerism, or Fascination, is the only cure that promises much relief; to those who wish information on the subject, I must refer Fascination, or the Philosophy of Charming. by J. B. Newman, published by Fowler & Wells, of this city.

Fever and Ague.

Take of cloves and cream of tartar, each half an ounce, and one ounce of peruvian bark, mix in a little tea, molasses or honey, and take it on the well days in such quantities as the stomach will bear.

Mumps.

This is a swelling, on the sides of the cheek and under the jaw, of the glands that produce saliva ; it sometimes renders swallowing and breathing difficult ; it goes off on the fourth day.

Flannel should be kept over the part, the diet light, and the bowels regular, with doses of castor oil ; when other organs are attacked, the treatment must be for inflammation of those organs.

Felon in the Eye.

Take of lime water and sal. ammoniac equal parts,

add a very little verdigris, enough to color it slightly, and use it as a wash; or,

Rub on the eye, with a soft hair pencil, the gall of an eel.

Fever Sore.

Take of horehound, low balm, sarsaparilla, loaf sugar, aloes, honey, gum camphor, spikenard, spirits of turpentine, each one ounce. Dose, one table-spoonful, three mornings, missing three; and for a wash, make a strong tea of sumach, washing the affected parts frequently, and keeping the bandage well wet; or,

Take two and a half drachms of blue vitriol, three drachms of alum, six drachms of loaf sugar, and put them into a pint of good vinegar, adding three table-spoonfuls of honey. This is an excellant wash for fever sores, and scrofulous humors.

Scurvy.

Take three ounces of nitre, and dissolve it in one quart of good vinegar. Dose, one table spoonful, if the stomach will bear it, if not take less.

Rattles in Children.

Powder an oz. of bloodroot fine, and give the child a tea-spoonful at a dose, repeating the operation three times. We have never known it to fail in curing this troublesome complaint.

Sick Headache.

Take a tea-spoonful of powdered charcoal in molasses every morning, and wash it down with a little tea; or,

Drink half a glass of raw rum or gin, and drink freely of mayweed tea.

Sprains.

Take of spirits of turpentine, proof brandy, neatsfoot oil, urine, and beef's gall, each one glass, adding one tea-spoonful of fine salt; mix, and simmer them together, and rub it on the affected parts as hot as can be borne; or,

Take one ounce of ginger, the whites of two eggs, and one tea-spoonful of fine salt; make these into a poultice and lay it on the parts affected.

Reduce a Swelling.

Take of rum half a pint, warm it, then add half an ounce of tinc. of camphor, half an ounce of laudanum, and put them into a bottle; and by frequently rubbing the parts affected with this mixture, hot as can be borne it will soon reduce the worst kind of swellings.

Ague.

Make a poultice of ginger and flour, and apply it warm to the face.

Falling of the Bowels, in Children.

Apply the oil of hen's eggs to the parts—put them n their proper place—then roast an egg, and lay it on as hot as can be borne.

Weak Limbs.

Take the shavings of leather, and cumfrey root equal parts, steep them in proof brandy, and use it as a wash.

Hiccough.

Take five drops of the oil of amber in mint tea, every ten minutes, untill they cease.

Boils.

Make a poultice of ginger and flour, and lay it on the boil; this will soon draw it to a head.

Pains.

Steep marigold in good cider-vinegar, and frequently wash the affected parts; this will afford speedy relief; or
Take half a pound of tar, and half a pound of tobacco, and boil them down separately to a thick substance, then simmer them together; spread a plaster, and apply it to the affected parts, and it will afford immediate relief.

Urinary Obstructions.

Steep pumpkin seeds in gin, and drink about three glasses a day; or,
Administer half a drachm of uva ursi, every morning, and a dose of paregoric every evening.

Ear-Ache.

Roast a piece of lean mutton, squeeze out the juice and drop it into the ear as hot as it can be borne; or,
Roast an onion, and put it into the ear, as hot as it can be borne.

Catarrh.

Take the bark of sassafras root. dry and pound it, use it as a snuff, taking two or three pinches a day.

Cramp in the Stomach.

Take ten drops of lavender on sugar, and repeat the dose every ten minutes, until relieved.

Callus.

Take of brandy, pig's-foot oil, beef's gall, and spirits of turpentine, each one gill; simmer all together, and rub on the parts, as hot as can be borne, about three times a day.

Palpatation of the Heart.

This disease consists in a vehement and irregular motion of the heart, and is induced by organic affections, a morbid enlargement of the heart itself, or of the large vessels, a diminution of the cavities of its ventricles from inflammation or other causes, polypi, ossification of the aorta or other vessels, plethora, debility or mobility of the system, malconformation of the thorax, and many of the causes inducing syncope.

During the attacks the motion of the heart is performed with greater rapidity, and generally with more force than usual, which is not only to be felt with the hand, but may often be perceived by the eye, and in a few instances even be heard; there is frequently a purplish hue of the lips and cheeks, and a great variety of anxious and painful sensations.

In some instances the complaint has terminated in death, but in many others it is merely symptomatic of hysteria and other nervous disorders.

In the treatment of this disease, it should be our study, if possible, to find out the exciting cause, and to remove this. If it arises from plethora, bleeding with purgatives should be adopted; if from debility, bitters with chalybeates and cold bathing, &c. will be proper; when symptomatic of any nervous disorder, œther, castor, musk, and other antispasmodics, conjoined with tonics, will be advisable.

As the disease, however, arises from an organic affection of the heart itself in many instances, or of the aorta, or other large vessels connected with it, all that may be in our power in such cases will be to caution the patient against exposing herself or himself to such circumstances as may increase the action of the sanguiferous system, particularly fits of passion, sudden surprises, violent exercise, or great exertions of the body.

Menstrual Discharges. (See *Fem. Obstruct.*)

In order to check the too free discharge, take of

burnt alum, three drachms, dragon's blood one drachm; and make into pills. Dose, four or five, night and morning; or,

Make a tea of snake weed, or yarrow, and drink freely; or,

In order to help the discharge, take one tea-spoonful of the tincture of gum guaiacum in a tumbler of new milk on going to bed, two or three nights before the full of the moon; and at the same time, make a strong tea of snakeroot, and drink in the course of the day as much as the stomach will bear. This may be depended upon as an infallible remedy.

Chilblains.

Wash the parts in strong alum water, applied as hot as can be borne.

Corns.

Spread a plaster made of gum ammoniac, and lay it over the corn; or,

Boil tobacco down to an extract, then mix with it a quantity of white-pine pitch; and apply it to the corn, renewing it once a week until the corn disappears.

Jaundice.

Take whites of two hen's eggs, beat them up well in a gill of water; take this, a little every morning; it will soon do good; it also creates an appetite, and strengthens the stomach;

Take the yoke of a hen's egg, a tea-spoonful of lemon juice, a tea-spoonful of sugar; mix; take this three mornings, and then miss three; repeat it if necessary: or,

Take of black cherry-three bark, two ounces; bloon root and goldthread, each half an ounce; put into a pint of brandy. Dose, from a tea-spoonful to a table-spoonful, morning and night.

FAMILY PHYSICIAN.

Itch.

Take a 1-4 lb. hog's lard, 2 oz. turpentine, 1 oz. flour sulphur, and mix them together thoroughly. Apply it to the wrists, knees, ancles, and elbows, and rub it on the palms of the hands if there are any raw spots. Continue it three or four nights and a cure is accomplished.

Sore Legs.

Apply to the sore a batch of common tow, and keep it wet with new milk; or,

Take wormwood, smart-weed, blue vervine; boil in weak lye; apply with a soft brush or feather.

Monthly Course—Painful.

Take a teaspoonful of flax-seed three times a day.

Raising Blood.

Make a tea of white oak bark, and drink freely during the day; or,

Take half a pound of yellow dock'root, boil in new milk, say one quart; drink one gill three times a day; and take one pill of white pine pitch every day, to heal the wound or leak.

Strengthening Plaster.

Take of tar and hemlock gum, equal parts; stir in a tea-spoonful of sulphur: it is fit for use.

Bite of Poisonous Creatures.

Snake.—Apply juice of onions mixed with fine salt; or apply Spanish flies, until a blister is raised.

Mad dog.—Take two table-spoonfuls of fresh chloride of lime; mix with water; wash the wound often.

Bites or Stings.—Make a strong tincture of lobelia, and apply it often; this is an infallible cure.

Deafness.

Take ants' eggs and onion juice; mix, and drop into the ear; or,

Drop into the ear, at night, six or eight drops of warm chamber lye.

Stomach Sickness.

Drink three or four times a day, of the steep made from the bark of white poplar roots.

Bleeding at the Lungs.

Take three or four drops of oil of golden rod.

Scrofula—Humor.

Administer one drachm of Peruvian bark; half in the morning and half at night; also, give the patient twenty drops of the oil of tar, at eleven o'clock, A. M. and four o'clock, P. M.

Take of powdered egg-shells one tea-spoonful, (or oyster-shells,) mixed with Peruvian bark, one eighth part, two or three times a day.

Bloody Urine.

Dissolve one ounce of gum Arabic in one gill of water; in a glass of this, drop in ten drops of vitriol oil; take of it two or three times a day.

Numb Palsy.

Take of ether, four ounces; oil of lavender, half an ounce; rub this mixture on; give one tea-spoonful when you commence the application, night and morning.

Nervous Affections—Sick Headache.

Make a tea of mullen seed and drink freely; or,

Take powdered charcoal (one tea-spoonful) in molasses, every day; wash it down with a little tea. This is good for sick headache; or,

Take three or four drops of nitric acid, in half a tumbler of cold water.

White Swelling.

Draw a blister on the inside of the leg, below the knee; keep it running with ointment made of hen manure—by simmering it in hog's lard with onions; rub the knee with the following kind of ointment; bits of peppermint, oil of sassafras, checkerberry, juniper, one drachm each; simmer in half a pint of neat's foot oil: rub on the knee three times a day.

Salt Rheum

Make a strong tea of elm root bark; drink the tea freely; and wash the affected part in the same; or,

Take one ounce of blue flag root, steep it in half a pint of gin; take a tea-spoonful three times a day morning, noon, and night: and wash with the same: or,

Take one ounce of oil of tar, one drachm of oil of checker berry: mix. Take from five to twenty drops, morning and night, as the stomach will bear.

Cutting Teeth.

Make a necklace of the bean called Job's tears, and let the child wear it around its neck.

Dropsy.

Take of cream of tartar, borax, ginger, gum myrrh, each one ounce: put into one pint of best gin: take one table-spoonful three times a day: or,

Take one drachm powdered broom-seed, put into one and a half glass of wine: take it early in the morning, fasting, one or two days; or,

Take blue flag root, half a pound; elecampane root, half a pound; boil in two gallons of water, down to one quart; add one pint of molasses and half a pint of gin. Take a wine-glassful three times a day; or,

Take as much as the stomach will bear, (say about a wine-glass,) of the inner bark of common elder in strong wine, morning, noon, and night.

Bilious Complaints.

Take dandelion (root and branch) and poplar tree root, each half a pound; steep out all the strength; simmer it down thick; add molasses, and take one tea-spoonful four times a day: or,

Take a quarter of a pound of black cherry-tree bark, one ounce of bloodroot; steep in a pint and a half of brandy three days; then add one gill of water and one gill of molasses; let it steep three days, and it is fit for use. Dose, from a table-spoonful to half a wine-glassful two or three times a day; if it should brace the stomach too much, take less; if not, take a little more.

Bilious Cholic.

Mix two table-spoonfuls of Indian meal in half a pint of cold water; drink it in two draughts; or,

Take W. I. rum, molasses, hog's fat, wine, each one gill; mix all together, and take it at discretion.

Humors.

Take saffron and Seneca snakeroot, equal parts; make a strong tea: drink half a pint per day, and this will drive out all humors from the system.

St. Anthony's Fire.

Dissolve two ounces of saltpetre in one pint of water; take from one tea-spoonful to a table-spoonful night and morning; wash in the same: or,

Take one glass of rum, and one glass spirits of turpentine : mix, and wash : and when the inflammation is gone, rub the parts with mutton tallow.

Dyspepsia.

Take back of white poplar root, boil it thick, add a little spirits : lay it on the stomach : or,
Take wintergreen and black cherry-tree bark, and yellow dock ; put into two quarts of water ; boil down to three pints ; take two or three glasses a day.

Sore and Weak Eyes.

Eye water: take white vitriol, one ounce : bray salt, one ounce : pour on a quart of boiling lime water ; let it settle, and it is fit for use ; or if too strong, weaken with lime water.
Use the *Harlem oil*, according to directions ; or,
Take white vitriol, one ounce ; sugar of lead, one ounce ; gunpowder, two ounces ; put into one quart of lime water ; let it settle twenty-four hours, and it is then fit for use.

Gout.

Dissolve half an ounce of camphor in three ounces of alcohol ; add one gill of boiling water ; rub it on as hot as can be borne ; or,
Take oil of lavender, half an ounce ; Sul. ether, four ounces ; alcohol, two ounces. Rub on the affected parts ; you will soon find relief.

Polypus.

Take two ounces of bloodroot, two drachms of cinnamon, two ounces of coak root, one drachm of borax, ten grains of sublimate ; mix together, and take four or five pinches, as a snuff, per day ; when it grows small, snuff up a little beet juice ; this will oftentimes blow it out or,

Take of bloodroot one part: shunk cabbage, half a part: lobelia, one part: Corr. sublimate, five grains; snakeroot, two parts: slippery elm, three parts: common snuff, one part: take a pinch four times a day.

Croup. No. 2.

Apply a plaster of yellow snuff to the throat; take a little physic; soak your feet in hot water, and apply onion poultice to your feet; or,

Take ten grains of white vitriol, ten drops of oil of vitriol, one ounce lime water; mix; take from five to twenty drops every hour; lay a plaster of yellow snuff on the throat; and when you think the bladder is almost full, give a vomit of bloodroot and lobelia, equal parts; this will cause the bladder to break, and the child will be cured.

Felon on the Hand.

Take of blue flag-root and hellebore equal parts; boil in milk and water; soak the hand in this, as hot as you can bear it, say twenty minutes; then bind the roots on your fingers one hour, and a cure will be the result.

Rupture.

Rub on angle-worm ointment, morning and evening, make a plaster of the yolk of three eggs, mixed with a gill of brandy; simmer together, and use it as a plaster: at the same time drink freely of white oak bark tea, and keep up your rupture with a good truss.

Flour Albus.

Put one ounce of borax into a pint of wine: take half a wine-glass three times a day: and drink a tea made of hackmetack bark.

St. Vitus's Dance.

Purge with fleur d'luce; then take camphor and bloodroot, and steep them in spirit; take a tea-spoonful three times a day; then take a tea made of sage, rue, pennyroyal; drink freely; or,

Pour cold water, from the height of four or five feet on the patient's head, three or four times a day; at the same time, take of ether one ounce; oil of lavender one drachm; mix and rub on the wrists and back of the neck a tea-spoonful night and morning.

Gravel, or Stone.

Take of lobelia, violets, camomile cleavers, smartweed, each one ounce; boil in two quarts of water down to one quart; add one quart of common lye, one quart of Holland gin. 'Dose, drink half a pint per day, and at night take half a wine-glassful, and the same quantity of onion juice, when going to bed; drink nettle tea for a common drink; or,

Use Harlem oil, according to directions; or,

Take spirits of turpentine, sweet spirits of nitre, oil of juniper, balsam of sulphur, each half an ounce; mix; and take fifteen drops in a strong tea made from the bark of the high blackberry bush. Drink a tea made from horsemint, freely, as a common drink; or,

Take castile soap, eight ounces; quick lime, one ounce; oil of tartar, one drachm; mix into five-grain pills, and take three or four per day: or,

Make of bean leaves a strong tea, and drink freely; or,

Take of uvi ursa any quantity; powder it fine. Dose, from half a drachm to a whole drachm, morning, noon and night.

Urinary Discharges (too free.)

Take two ounces of Peruvian bark; steep it in one quart of wine twenty-four hours; add two drachms of alum. Dose, from a spoonful to a wine-glassful two or three times a day.

Liver Complaint.

Drop into a quart of cold water aquafortis enough to make it a pleasant sour, and drink (through a quill, on account of the teeth) freely through the day; or,

Take of tincture of guaiacum and oil of tar, each one ounce, mixed. Dose, from five to twenty drops.

Rub on the side, oil of lavender one drachm, ether two ounces, oil of sassafras one drachm.

Mortification.

Make a strong decoction of white oak bark; thicken with powdered charcoal and Indian meal; and apply it to the parts affected. Try it every two hours; or,

Make a strong tea from Indigo weed, bathe the part affected till well.

Wen.

Take clean linen rags; burn them on a pewter plate, wipe off the oil on lint, and lay the lint on the wen; it will soon drop out of itself; or,

Take equal parts of alum and salt; simmer them together, and wash the parts three or four times a day.

Whooping Cough.

Take of sweet oil, garlic, onions, each a gill; simmer together half an hour; then add a glass of honey, a tea-spoonful of paregoric, and a tea-spoonful of tincture of camphor. Dose, one tea-spoonful three or four times a day; or,

Take of elecampane, four ounces; honey, half a pound; set it in a warm place until it forms a syrup. Dose, one tea-spoonful three times a day.

Worms.

Take one ounce of powdered snake-head (herb,) one drachm of aloes, and one drachm of prickly ash bark, powder these, and to half a tea-spoonful of this powder add a tea-spoonful of boiling water, and a tea-spoonful of molasses, and take this as a dose, night or morning, more or less, as the symptoms require; or,

Take tobacco leaves, pound them up with honey, and lay them on the belly of the child, or grown person, at the same time administering a dose of some good physic; or,

Take garden parsley; make into a tea; and let the patient drink freely of it; or,

Take the scales that fall around the blacksmith's anvil, powder them fine, and put them in some sweetened rum. Shake them when you take them, and give a tea-spoonful three times a day.

Toothache.

Make an extract from white poplar bark; mix with it a litte rum; put into your tooth, and you will soon find relief; or,

Take the bark of white poplar roots, boil it down to the thickness of tar; take a tea-spoonful of this extract, put into a glass of spirit, shake it well, and apply to the tooth.

Week Stomach.

Take of gum mastic, and spermaceti, each two ounces; melt them together over a slow fire, then stir in brown sugar, say two pounds, make into small balls, size of a walnut, and take three per day on an empty stomach; or,

Take garden wormwood, tansy, balm of Gilead buds, buds of pitch pine, each half an ounce, step in one quart of spirits. Dose, form a table-spoonful to half a wine-glassful, morning and evening.

Ringworms.

Boil three figs of tobacco in one pint of urine, add

one gill of vinegar, and one gill of lye; and rub this wash on frepuently; or,

Take carbold and pulverize it fine, mix it with gin, and apply it with a feather.

Cancer.

Boil down the inner bark of white and red oak, to the consistency of molasses; apply as a plaster, shifting it once a week; or,

Burn red oak bark to ashes; sprinkle it on the sore, till it is eaten out, and then apply a plaster of tar; or,

Take garget berries, and leaves of stramonium; simmer them together, in equal parts of neat's foot oil and the tops of cicuta or hemlock; mix well together, and apply it to the parts affected; at the same time make a tea of wintergreen (root and branch;) put about a handful into two quarts of water; add two ounces of sulphur of brimstone, and drink of this tea freely during the day.

Diabetes.

Take of loaf sugar, rosin and alum, equal parts; and take as much as the point of a penknife will contain three times a day; or,

Steep one ounce of ginger in one pint of good wine, and drink two or three glasses a day; or,

Dissolve in one quart of proof brandy, one ounce of spruce gum, and half an ounce of ginger. Dose, from one table-spoonful to half a wine-glassful, three times a day.

Bowel Complaints in Children.

Take of prepared chalk one ounce, tinct. of kino one ounce, Epsom salts one ounce, and water one pint; mix all well together and shake well before using. Dose, for a child one year of age, one table-spoonful morning, noon and night, and increase the dose as the symptoms may require.

Gravel. (*See Stone.*)

Make a strong tea of the herb called heart's ease, and drink freely; or,

Make of Jacob's ladder a strong tea, and drink freely.

Painter's Cholic.

Make of tartaric acid a syrup similar to that of lemon syrup; add a sufficient quantity of water, and drink two or three glasses a day.

Piles.

Take one ounce of garget root, and one ounce of burdock root, put them into a pint of boiling water, and let it steep awhile; when cool, add a little gin to prevent its souring, bottle it tight, and take from two to four table-spoonfuls daily; or,

Simmer sunflower seeds in cream, and make it into an ointment; and rub this ointment on the inside and outside, and for an injection use strong Castile soap-suds; or,

Take equal parts of the pitch of white pine and fir-balsam, make this into pills, and take four or five per day; or,

Take the Harlem Oil, according to the directions; or,

If external, rub on linseed oil; or, if internal, take a tea-spoonful of the same, three times a day; or,

Take of sulphur one ounce, hog's fat four ounces, strong tobacco-juice half a pint, and simmer them together into an ointment; and apply it.

Old and Inveterate Sores.

Take one ounce of copperas, two ounces of white vitriol, two ounces of rock-salt, two ounces of linseed oil, and eight ounces of molasses; boil them all together over a slow fire, and then add a pint of urine, and when cool, add half an ounce of the oil of vitriol, four ounces of the spirits of turpentine, and two ounces of the oil of tar; mix all well together, and the salve is fit for use.

Earache.

Take a table-spoonful of fine salt, and tie it up in a little bag, heat it quite hot, and lay it on the ear, shifting it several times; and it will afford speedy relief.

Convulsion Fits

May be cured by taking twenty drops of digitalis, ten at night and ten in the morning; and at the same time pour, in a small stream, about one quart of cold water from the height of two or three feet upon the fore part of the patient's head, and rub the back part of the neck with the following mixture: take of the oil of lavender two drachms, ether two ounces, alcohol one ounce; and when the fit is on, dash cold water in the patient's face as quick as possible, thus checking the spasms, and affording speedy relief.

Common Sore Throat.

Mix a glass of calcined magnesia with honey, and take one tea-spoonful every hour.

Epileptic Fits.

Take of the root of comfrey, sassafras, burdock, elecampane and horse-radish, and of hoarhoud, and raspberry leaves, equal parts; make these into a strong tea, and to an adult administer one gill, to a child a proportionably less quantity per day.

Sore Lips.

Wash the lips with a strong tea made from the bark of white oak.

Bleeding Piles.

Make a strong tea of yarrow, and drink freely; or, Take a piece of garget-root about the size of a hen's egg, put it into a pint of boiling water, and let it steep a few hours, when cool, take from one to three table spoonfuls, as the stomach will best bear daily, before eating.

Ulcer.

Boil the leaves of the walnut tree in soft water, and frequently wash the sore with it, keeping a cloth wet with the wash on the parts all the time.

Inward Ulcers.

Take of the bark of sassafras-root two ounces, blood-root one ounce, colt-foot two ounces, gum-myrrh one ounce, winter-bark one-ounce, and aloes one ounce, steep them together in two quarts of rum, let them steep awhile, and when cool, drink one glass every morning before eating.

Distress after Eating.

Take of soda two parts, and of rhubarb one part, mix them well together, and take an even tea-spoonful, fifteen minutes after eating, in water.

Warts. No. 2.

Make a strong solution of corrosive sublimate, and rub it on the warts two or three times a day.

Sore Nipples.

Spread a plaster of fir balsam, and apply it to the breast after the child has nursed.

Phthisic.

Take four ounces of hen's fat, and with it simmer a little of the root of skunk-cabbage. Dose, one tea-spoonful, three times a day.

Consumptive Cough, with Distress.

Take of the extract of cicuta one ounce, and oxide of zinc half an ounce; make them into a common sized pill, and take one night and morning.

Tape Worm.

Boil the stem of pomegranate very strong, and when cool, drink freely of the tea; or,

Take of spirits of turpentine and rum, each half a wine glass, and sweeten with molasses; take a little of this every hour, and afterwards take a smart dose of physic.

Vomiting Prevented.

Pour boiling water on a piece of camphor, and take one dessert-spoonful every ten minutes, until the vomiting ceases.

Taking Poisons.

1. When a person has through mistake taken *Oil of Vitriol*, administer large doses of magnesia, or soap and water.
2. *Tartar Emetic.* Let the patient drink a tea made from Peruvian bark, very strong.
3. *Saltpetre.* Give the patient one tea-spoonful of mustard seed in water, and after vomiting, give him a little laudanum.
4. *Laudanum.* Give a tea-spoonful of mustard seed, and increase the quantity, until it operates and keep the patient moving.
5. *Lunar Caustic.* Administer a tea-spoonful of common salt, at different times, until it operates.

6. *Corrosive Sublimate.* Take the white of eggs in water, until vomiting is produced, and apply slices of onions to all parts of the body.

7. And in any other case of the kind, administer a table-spoonful of powdered charcoal, and in fifteen minutes afterwards give a dose of physic.

Bleeding at the Stomach.

Take a table-spoonful of camomile tea every ten minutes until the bleeding stops.

Hoarseness.

Make a strong tea of horse-radish and yellow dock roots, sweeten with honey, and drink freely.

Windy Stomach.

Chew saffron leaves, and swallow the spittle.

Gleets.

Make of turpentine a four-grain pill, and take three a day.

Sweat.

Take of nitre half a drachm, snake's head (herb) one ounce, ipecac. half an ounce, saffron one ounce, camphor one ounce, snake-root one ounce, seneca-root one ounce, bark of sassafras-root one ounce, opium half an ounce; put the above into three quarts of Holland gin, and take a table-spoonful in catnip tea every ten minutes, until it produces a free sweat.

Humors.

For any kind of humors—take of checkerberry and the essence of tar, each one ounce, mix them well together, and give to an adult from five to fifteen drops, and to a child from three to ten drops, morning and evening; and at the same time, let the patient drink freely of juniper-tea; and if he chooses, he may take the drops in a little of this tea.

To procure Sleep.

Wash the head in a decoction of dill seed, and smel of it frequently.

King's Evil.

Take of antimony and salt, equal parts, melt them in a crucible one hour, let it cool, and then break the crucible and rub this composition with corrosive sublimate equal parts, until it be well mixed, then make into pills, and take from two to four a day; and take a portion of some good physic weekly.

Good Remedy for Fits.

Take of the tinct. of foxglove, ten drops at each time twice a day, and increase one drop at each time as long as the stomach will bear it, or it causes a nauseous feeling.

Strained Stomach.

Take of white-pine pitch and of sulphur, each a quarter of a pound, and of honey three ounces; simmer them well together, make into pills, and take four of these pills in the course of the day.

Stiffened Joints.

Take of the bark of white oak and sweet apple-trees, equal parts; boil them down to a thick substance, and then add the same quantity of goose-grease or oil, simmer all together, and then rub it on the parts warm.

Cough.

1-2 lb. liquorice root, same quantity brook liverwort, 2 oz. elecampane, 1-4 lb. Solomon's seal, 1-2 lb. spikenard, 1-4 lb. gumfire, add a gallon of water and boil it down to a quart, then add 2 lbs. strained honey and a pint old brandy. Dose, half a glass before each meal. This is the old Indian cure for a cold, and is among them considered infallible. Caution is necessary while using this compound to avoid exposure, for it is of such a warming nature that without it there is great danger to be apprehended.

Whites in Women.

Make a strong syrup of yarrow, and take from one table-spoonful to two thirds of a wine-glassful, three times a day.

Weeping Eyes.

Wash them in camomile tea, night and morning.

Spine Complaints.

Mix beef-gall with vinegar, and bathe the back with this wash night and morning.

Cure for Old Sores.

Take of copperas one ounce, white vitriol two ounces, salt two ounces, linseed oil two ounces, molasses eight ounces, and urine one pint; mix them well together, and then boil the mixture over a slow fire fifteen minutes; when cool, add one ounce of the oil of vitriol, and four ounces of the spirits of turpentine; and apply it to the sore with a soft brush.

Pimples.

Take a tea-spoonful of the tinct. of gum guaiacum, and one tea-spoonful of vinegar; mix, and apply it to the affected parts.

Cure for Toothache.

Mix alum and salt together; or powdered alum and spirits of ether; and apply it on a small wad to the affected tooth.

Lame Feet.

Take one pint of urine, one table-spoonful of fine salt, and one fig of tobacco; simmer strong, and apply it as a wash, as hot as can be borne every night; and when about to commence bathing the feet take one tea-spoonful of the tinct. of guaiacum; and in using the wash, if it should cause nausea, take one more tea-spoonful of the tincture, and cease bathing.

Frost Bite.

Dissolve half a pound of alum in one gallon of hot water, or less quantities in proportion; and apply with hot cloths laid on the parts, keeping them wet with the wash.

Burns.

Take of fir-balsam one ounce, sweet oil two ounces; mix, and apply with a feather, and then wet a cloth with it and lay it on the sore, keeping the cloth wet all the time.

Sore, or Weak Eyes.

Take of white vitriol ten drops, mix in lime water, and take from five to twenty drops, as the stomach will bear.

Hysterics.

Take the leaves of motherwort and thoroughwort, and the bark of poplar root equal parts, mix them in molasses, and take four of them when the first symptoms of the disorder are felt, and they will effectually check it.

Universal Cure-all.

I have thus named this valuable composition, at the suggestion of an eminent physician at the South, who, as his letter to me states, has through its instrumentality, in very many cases, performed some very remarkable cures. In his letter to me he says, "You state in your letter, that you paid thirty dollars for this recipe—but my opinion is, that on account of its great efficacy in the cure of some of the worst of complaints and diseases that the human flesh is heir too, it is a duty you owe to your fellow-creatures to make it a public thing. I am at a loss where to begin, in order to inform you of the many cases of positive and permanent cures that have come under my own observation in its use; I will at this time mention but two instances; the first being that of a lady, that had lost the entire use of her limbs, and who had not been able to either feed herself, or to walk a step for upwards of one year, was restored to perfect health and strength in about six weeks, by frequently rubbing different parts of her body with this composition; the quantity I prescribed during that time was about forty-eight ounces. The other case, was that of a young man, who had lost the use of his limbs, by a shock of the palsy, (as it was thought,) and who, after suffering for four years, was cured in a few weeks, by its use; the quantity I used in both of these cases weekly, was about six or eight ounces."

I have proved it to be a permanent cure in very many difficult cases; viz., in case of a young man, who had lost the use of his hand, and who by continuing its use for three days was completely cured. A woman who had suffernd much from weakness and debility after child-birth, was restored to perfect health and strength, by frequently rubbing her body with this composition in a few days.

Rubbing this composition on, and in the vicinity of the parts affected, will be found to be very efficacious in the liver complaint, consumption, broken breasts, sore or weck eyes, burns, (rubbing it around, but not on the sore, or the eye,) bilious or cramp cholic stoppages in the bowels (mixed with goose-oil, and then giving a little physic) chilblains, and by taking one or two tea-spoonfuls in a little sweetened tea, it will cure pains in the side, and stomach, and in short, it will be found efficacious in almost every kind of disease. The recipe is as follows: Take of the oil of lavender half an ounce, sulph. ether three ounces, alcohol one ounce, and laudanum two drachms; mix all well together, and it is fit for use.

Locked-jaw.

If the wound be occasioned by running a nail or something of the kind into the foot or hand, let the parts be well soaked in weak lye, and keep them bound up until the sore is quite healed; or,

When there is any appearance of the disease, let the patient take one table-spoonful of elixir, (See page 66,) in a wine-glassful of hot water. If this dose does not allay the symptoms, give the patient a thorough lobelia emetic. If the jaws become locked before the emetic is given, let the patient take half a table-spoonful of the tincture of lobelia seeds, and fill the spoon up with the elixir; and if the jaws are closed tight, put the above on one side of the mouth, and let it run down by the sides of the teeth and cheek; it will soon find way to the roots of the tongue, will relax the muscles, and the mouth will open without any force; and in fifteen minutes repeat the dose, giving, in half an hour afterwards, one tea-spoonful of vegetable powders, (See page 66,) in a tea-cupful of pennyroyal tea, this causes the patient to vomit, and to be relieved. If the spasms should continue, let this treatment be repeated.

MEDICAL PROPERTIES OF PLANTS.

Aloes.

It is cathartic, operating slowly, but certainly and has a particular affinity for the large intestines.

It slightly stimulates the stomach and is an excellent remedy in habitual costiveness, attended with torpor of the digestive organs, administered in minute doses. It is generally given in doses from five to fifteen grains. The best way, however, of administering it is in pills, combined with other articles.

Avens, or Chocolate Root.

An eminent physician observes, " that it is an excellent remedy in all cases of the first stage of consumption, and in debility." It is preferable to Peruvian bark in the cure of intermittents, dysentery, chronic diarrhœa, wind, cholic. affections of the stomach, asthmatic symptoms, and in all cases of debility, whites, flooding, sore throat.

It is good for fevers. After the proper evacuations, it may be given till the fever is broken up. The doses are daily, a pint of weak decoction, or about sixty grains of the powder, devided into three equal parts, and mixed with honey. It is good for the cure of salt rheum, and scaled head ; make a strong tea of the root, and drink freely ; and wash the humor frequently every day.

Arrow Head.

Made into a strong decoction, it is good as a drink, and as a wash, in case of being bit by a mad dog.

Black Snakeroot.

It is an astringent, promotes urinary evacuations, and general healthy action. aids menstrual discharges, is efficacious in removing pains, sickness of the stomach, and heartburn in pregnancy. Administer it in tea; take two ounces of the root, add a pint of boiling water, keep it in a warm place, and drink occasionally two or three swallows at a time, through the day. It may be used in connection with slippery elm before child-birth, as it generally assists nature in such cases. It is excellent in bowel complaints, especially in children.

Blackberry Root.

This root mixed with gold-thread, and boiled down strong; is a sure remedy for canker in the mouth, throat or stomach; wash the mouth with it, and take inwardly a table-spoonful daily. It will give great relief in cases of gravel and dysentery, if taken often during the day.

Black Alder Bark.

A syrup made from it is good for indigestion and it is good for jaundice. The tags of it, are good (as a wash) for all kinds of spontaneous swellings. The bark powdered is good for worms. Dose, half a teaspoonful in molasses.

Blood Root.

It is excellent in coughs and croup. It is an emetic, and narcotic; produces perspiration, and menstrual discharges; is good in influenza, hooping cough, and phthisic. It is good in bilious complaints, combined with Black cherry-tree bark, also in cases of scarlet fever and in catarrh.

Butter, or Oil Nut.

Extract from the bark makes a mild cathartic, like

rhubarb. It is good in costiveness and dysentery. Dose from fifteen to thirty grains.

Butter-cup, or Crow's foot.

It is good for drawing blisters, for corns on the feet, and made into a tea, it is excellent in cases of asthma.

Blue Flag Root.

This root has effected wonderful cures in aggravated rhumatic complaints. Give, after eating, a tea-spoonful, three times a day, of a decoction of the root made into a tincture (by putting one oz. of the dried root into half a pint of gin;) decrease the quantity if slight pains in the head or breast are produced. It is excellent in removing humor from the system—much more so than the outrageous mercury, and much more safe. For a cathartic take half a tea-spoonful of the powder in molasses.

Camomile.

Used as a tea, it is good for relieving the stomach in cases of vomiting, and steeped strong, it stops bleeding in the stomach.

Caraway.

When steeped in water it is very good for children, to remove wind from the bowels.

Carrots.

Boiled in milk and water and applied as a poultice to old sores, it is excellent. Bathe the sore well with the liquor before applying the poultice: it draws out all inflammation.

Checkerberry.

It is good for salt-rheum simmered with neat's foot oil and rubbing it on the parts affected.

Canada Snake Root.

It is aromatic, stimulant and tonic; very good for catarrh and pain in the stomach, coughs, colds, and pulmonary complaints.

Red Cedar.

The oil, combined with oil of spearmint, is good for gravel, disease of the kidneys, scalding of the urine. Combined with sarsaparilla, yellow dock, and burdock, and made into a syrup, adding to a pint of this syrup one ounce of gum guaiacum, it is very good in all venereal complaints. Dose from a table-spoonful to a wine-glass, as you can best bear. The berries simmered in neat's foot oil are good ointment for rheumatism, lame back, &c.

Catnip.

Steeped and sweetened with loaf sugar, it is good for sore throats; mixed with fresh butter and sugar, good for fresh wounds, swelled bowels in children, by bathing; it is also useful in fevers, producing perspiration without increasing the heat of the body.

Comfrey.

It is a mucilage, well adapted to allay irritation; good in dysentery, diarrhœa, consumptive complaints, and coughs.

Currants.

A tea made of the leaves of this bush is good in dropsical complaints; and taken as a common drink, it promotes a free passage for the discharge of the urine; it is also good for the stone or gravel.

Dandelion.

The root and branch of this plant should be steeped

in soft water a sufficient length of time to extract all its virtues; then strain the liquor and simmer until it becomes quite thick; and then, for all bilious complaints, from one to three glasses a day may be taken with decidedly beneficial effects. It can also be made into pills. It is a good medicine for complaints of the liver, dropsy, &c.

Dragon's Claw, or Fever Root.

It is useful in fevers, as it keeps up a moisture of the skin, without producing excitement To one tea-spoonful of the root, add half a pint of boiling water, and drink freely when it is blood-warm.

Dwarf Elder Berries.

They are excellent in rheumatic and dropsical complaints, also in cases of swollen limbs. The berries must be steeped in spirits, and taken in small doses just before eating.

Elecampane.

It is used in cases of suppression of the menses, diseases of the chest, and general debility arising from weakness in the digestive organs; it is also useful in dropsy. Of the decoction, one or two fluid ounces may be taken at a time. It is sometimes used in coughs, and pulmonary affections.

Elder Blows, Bark and Berries.

The flowers are good for the scurvey, taken in a strong tea; for bowel complaints in children they are excellent. They are laxative, and purify the blood; are also good for the gout, steeped in vinegar and salt, a table-spoonful mixed with the vinegar, rubbed on as hot as the patient can bear it. For erysipelas it is good steeped in vinegar and rum; also for St. Anthony's fire; add a spoonful of fine salt to a pint of the steep; take a spoonful, and at the same time bathe the parts.

Foxglove.

It produces a free discharge of urine, is good in dropsy of the chest, reduces inflammation by lessening the action of the heart, reduces frequency of the pulse; is good in consumptive complaints; especially inflammation of the lungs. It is a poison, and too large a dose will produce spasms, vertigo and death. A dose of the powder is one grain, to be taken two or three times a day, and gradually increased untill it affects the head, stomach, pulse or kidneys. It is said to be of use in case of convulsion fits; and made into an ointment, it helps scrofula sores.

Fir Balsam.

It is good for sore nipples, flour albus, fresh wounds and weakness of the stomach. Dose, twenty or thirty drops taken on loaf sugar, molasses, or anything most convenient.

Fever Root.

It is good in the typhus fever as well as others; keeping the skin moist without producing excitement. To a tea-spoonful of the powdered root, add half a pint of boiling water, and drink freely.

Ginger.

It is good in cholic, pain in the stomach, dyspepsia; promotes perspiration, warms the whole system. It is, prepared with gentian root, an excellent stomach powder. Dose, one ounce of gentian root and one drachm of ginger, mixed together, and take a spoonful in molasses every morning.

Golden Thread.

It is a tonic, promoting digestion, and is good for dyspepsia and sore mouth. Combined with camomile, it is good for sore lips, chapped hands, and chilblains on the feet ; mixed with black cherry-tree bark it is good for jaundice.

Garlic.

Draughts made of garlics, and applied to the feet at night, are good to remove feverish symptoms and equalize the circulations. It is very good in all inflammatory diseases ; also for discussing indolent tumors, coughs, colds, asthma.

Gentian.

It is a valuable tonic, excites the appetite, invigorates the system, and increases moderately the temperature of the body. It is good for debility of the digestive organs, gout, hysteria. scrofula and dyspepsia. Dose, from ten to forty grains.

Gum Arabic.

It is nutritive, and soothing to irritated parts ; good to prevent bleeding in dysentery, hoarseness, whooping cough, and suppression of urine. Take a handful of English barly, gum Arabic, a piece about the size of a walnut, with a little slippery-elm ; pour upon it a pint of boiling water, steep it and sweeten with loaf sugar. This is excellent where the patient has not much appetite and cannot bear solid food.

Horse Radish.

It promotes appetite, and invigorates the digestive powers. It is useful in hoarseness, when made into a syrup.

Hyssop.

It is very useful in producing expectoration, or discharge of mucus from the lungs, for catarrh, especially in old people, and as a gargle in sore throats. Make a tea, and drink at discretion.

Hops.

Hops are tonic, good in dysentery, nervous tremors, weakness and tremors of inebriates. A pillow made of hops wet with rum, is good to produce sleep, and allay nervous irritation, good in after-pains of women and valuable in fermentations.

Hoarhound.

It strengthens the lungs; a cold tea of it is good to prevent children from coughing, and loosens phlegm in the stomach. Mixed with colt's foot, it is fine for lung complaints.

Hemlock. (Bark.)

It is a powerful astringent. It is good for a bath in cases of falling of the body, falling of the womb, weak joints, &c. When the bath is used, about one third of brandy ought to be added. The gum, mixed with Burgundy pitch, makes an excellent plaster.

Iceland Moss.

It is good for a cough. It is bracing and nourishing.

Indian Hemp.

It is one of the best remedies for the palpatation of the heart that is to be found, and it is a powerful nervine, very good in old standing nervous complaints of women.

Take an even tea-spoonful of the powdered root, in molasses, three or four times a day, for a few weeks.

It is a fine substitute for opium without its *effects*, or tendency to costiveness and inaction.

Juniper Bush.

Its berries are a very excellent counter-poison, and also a great resister of pestilence. They are efficacious in the cure of wounds occasioned by the bite or sting of any beast or serpent of a poisonous nature. They are very good in cases of urinary suppressions, and strangury. A lye made from the ashes and used as a drink, will cure the dropsy. They expel wind, strengthen the stomach and eyesight, repress fluxes, good for piles, palsy, and falling sickness. Eating eight or ten of the berries every morning fasting, is good for a bad cough, shortness of breath, and consumptive complaints.

Knot Grass.

The juice of this herb or grass is excellent to stop bleeding at the nose or stomach—being of a very cooling nature. Made into powder and taken in wine it is a remedy in case of being bitten by any venomous creature. It is also good to expel worms. It is also said to be a sovereign remedy in all cases of inflammation, gangrene, canker, ulcer, broken joints and ruptures, and dysentery.

Lobelia.

It must be dried, pulverized, put into bottles, and very tightly corked—otherwise, its strength will soon evaporate. This herb, if properly administered, will invariable break up diseases of very long standing. By its powerful action upon the great sympathetic nerve, it allays irritation and inflammation; it is peculiarly adapted to the following cases, viz. cholera, hydrophobia, bite of rabid animals, lockjaw, asthma, fits, spasmodic affections, whooping cough, tightness in the chest, difficulty in breathing, bilious complaints, and consumption.

Lobelia will penetrate and equalize the system, remove all obstruction, cleanse the stomach and bowels, purify the blood, remove disease from the lungs and the liver, in a manner far superior to what calomel ever could, or ever will do. Dose, one tea-spoonful at a time—sometimes it requires two or three, depending upon the constitution of the patient, and the nature of the disease.

When taken as an emetic, mix it with an equal quantity of blood-root. This is fine in case of bilious cholic. When made into a pill, dampen it with balsam capiva, adding a small quantity of Castile soap. Take three pills for a dose, and if the patient does not obtain speedy relief, repeat the dose in about six minutes. By applying the powdered herb to an aching tooth, it will soon afford relief. A tincture made from lobelia, is an excellent remedy in case of being stung by a bee or wasp, and is good in all kinds of poisonous affections, venereal complaints, St. Anthony's fire, &c.

Liquorice.

It is good for a cough. Take a large tea-spoonful of linseed oil, one ounce of stick liquorice, four ounces of best raisens, put the ingredients into two quarts of soft water, boil this down to one quart, then add a quarter of a pound of brown sugar, and one table-spoonful of lemon juice. Drink half a pint of this on going to bed, and take a swallow or two when your cough is troublesome day and night.

Lady's Slipper.

The root of this plant has a tendency to lessen the animal energy, and to allay nervous affections, and is anti-spasmodic. It may be used in all cases instead of valerian; and is also in most cases far preferable to opium, as it is destitute of any narcotic effect. It promotes sleep, and allays the headache. Dose, one tea-spoonful in warm water, adding a little sugar.

Liverwort.

The root is excellent in all diseases of the liver, inflammation, yellow jaundice, chronic coughs; and will check the spread of ring-worms and running sores. Made into beer and drank freely, it will reduce the heat of the liver and kidneys. It is both cleansing and cooling.

Motherwort.

It is excellent in all nervous and hypochondriacal affections, dizziness in the head, &c. A strong tea, made of it and drank freely, will raise the spirits and impart new life and vigor to the whole system.

Mosses.

The ground moss, bruised and boiled in water, will ease all inflammation and pain caused by heat. Tree moss is also of a cooling, modifying, digesting nature. The powder of this moss, taken in a drink, is good for the dropsy, and strengthens the sinews; and, with oil of roses, will cure the headache. Stone moss is good in the cure of the phthisic and asthma, by making into a tea and drinking freely.

Mullen.

Steep the leaves in vinegar, and it is good for a lame side, and internal bruises. The centre leaves, steeped in milk and sweetened with sugar, are excellent for dysentery, especially in children. With strawberry-leaves and cleavers, steeped, it is good in cases of kidney complaints and obstructions of the urine.

Mouse Ear.

This herb is one of the best things known for the dysentery. Boil a handful of the leaves in milk and water, sweeten it with loaf sugar, and drink it freely.

Mustard (Garden).

It promotes digestion, creates appetite, removes pain from the stomach and bowels. The white mustard is good for dyspepsia; it may be taken whole, a tea-spoonful being the usual dose. It is good applied to the feet as draughts; it is also often used in cases where blistering is said to be needed. A tea-spoonful of the seed is good for the cholic; a tea-spoonful of the seed bruised, acts as an emetic; a tea-spoonful of the seed powdered, and taken in warm water, will expel poison from the stomach very promptly.

Prickly Ash.

The bark and berries are very stimulating, tonic, and invigorating. It is good for chronic rheumatism, for the toothache, scrofulous humors, and ulcerated sore legs.

Pennyroyal.

It is gently stimulant, and will produce universal perspiration if taken in large quantities hot. It is considered one of the best medicines in sudden suppression of the menses, prepared in the following manner; take an even tea-spoonful of black pepper powdered fine, put it into a tumbler of this tea, and drink when going to bed, after soaking the feet in weak lye; this remedy is almost infallible.

Plantain.

If poisoned by dogwood, boil plantain strong, and wash in the tea; if poisoned by ivy, do the same; and if you have an old sore do the same.

Quassia.

It is a well known tonic as well as bitter, and is

universally employed in medicine. It is a large, lofty tree, and strongly resembles our common ash; the leaves are of a bright red color, and every part of the tree is very bitter.

Poplar Bark (Root).

It is a sovereign remedy for the toothache: take the bark of the root, boil it in water down to an extract, mix with a little spirit, and put it into your tooth, and it performs a speedy cure in nine cases out of ten. A plaster, made in like manner, will cure the rheumatism, or any other pain.

Sassafras.

The bark cures the chronic rheumatism, is good for inward ulcers, sores, dropsy. With a tincture of the bark of the root, wash the sore, and if it smarts badly wash round it until you can bear to have it applied to the sore. It is good for cuts, or green wounds; dress the wound and keep it wet with this tincture, and in about ten days you will find it entirely or very nearly healed.

Sumach

The bark of the root, and berries, are good for canker in the mouth or throat. Make it into a strong tea, and wash the throat and mouth with it. A strong tea made with both bark and root sweetened with honey, will cure a cough, and has been known to cure a consumption.

Smart Weed.

This herb or plant is one of the most powerful suborifics, or swelling-remedies that I ever used. It is an excellent help in breaking up a fever. It can be made into a tea and drank freely at any time

Spikenard.

This is said to be a valuable remedy in cases of all kinds of sores and ulcers; and is very good in coughs and colds.

Thorn Apple.

It is used for cancerous sores, rheumatism, and spasmodic asthma, it makes an excellent ointment for the piles, or burns. By using the root, in smoking it with a pipe, it helps to breathe easy, and has cured many cases of asthma, after every other remedy has failed.

MEDICAL PREPARATIONS.

Elixir.

This elixir is made by adding one pound of best gum myrrh, and three ounces of African cayenne, to one gallon of alcohol, or fourth proof brandy. It may be taken from a tea-spoonful to a table-spoonful at a time, in water sweetened with molasses or sugar. It is efficacious in very many diseases used either internally or externally; especially in colds, coughs, consumption, pains in the bowels or stomach, rheumatism, inflammations, headache, toothache, cramp, cold feet, &c.

Vegetable Powder.

Take one pound of baberry bark, eight ounces of ginger, three ounces of cayenne, and four ounces of hemlock bark; mix, and for a dose, take one teaspoonful.

LADIES'

DOMESTIC ECONOMY

AND

HOUSEKEEPERS' GUIDE:

CONTAINING A SELECTION OF

VALUABLE FAMILY RECIPES,

MANY OF WHICH HAVE NEVER BEEN BEFORE PUBLISHED.

BY AN EXPERIENCED COOK.

New-York:
H. DAYTON, 36 HOWARD STREET;
INDIANAPOLIS, IND.: ASHER & CO.
1860.

CONTENTS.

Cakes, Bread, Yeast, &c.

A
	Page.
Apple Snow	96

B.
Baker's Ginger Bread	80
Best Cup Cake	85
Breakfast Butter Cakes	83
Brown, or Dyspepsia Bread	97
Buckwheat Cakes	83
Butter Cakes for Tea	83

C
Cake without Eggs	94
Common Plum Cake	82
Composition Cake	82
Cream Cup Cake	104
Cream Cake	83
Cream Cake, No. 2	86
Cake, Rich small-	75

D
Dyspepsia Cake	84
Dough Nuts	75
Dyspepsia Bread	81

G
Ginger Bread	85
Ginger Nuts	95
Ginger Snaps	95
Good Family Cake	95
Green Corn Cake	80

H
| Hard Wafers | 84 |
| Hoe Cake | 96 |

I
| Icing for Cakes | 85 |

	Page.
Indian Cakes	84
Indian Corn Cakes	96
Indian Griddle Cakes	82

J
| Jelly Cake | 95 |
| Jumbles | 95 |

L
Lemon Cake	94
Light Cake to be baked in Cups	82
Loaf Cake	84
Lemon Pie	81

M
Measure Cake	85
Molasses Dough Cake	80
Muffins	80

N
| New-York Cup Cake | 94 |

P
Plain Indian Cakes	83
Plum Cake	103
Pound Cake	82

R
Rich Jumbles	96
Rolls	84
Rye and Indian Bread	98
Rice Waffles	81

S
Seed Cakes	85
Savoy Cakes	81
Sugar Ginger Bread	85
Symbals	86

T
| Tea Cake, No. 1 | 83 |

CONTENTS.

Y
	Page
Yeast—to make it good	87
do —Milk	87
do of Cream Tartar and Salæratus	96

Pies, Preserves, Jellies, Sauce, &c.

A
Apple Sauce	96
Arrow Root Custard	85

B
Barberries—to Preserve	86
Black Currant Jelly	83
Blanc-Mange	84

C
Calf's-foot Jelly	87
Conserve Roses	86
Currant Jelly	88
Curries	79
Curry Powder	80

D
Damsons—to Preserve	102

F
Family Mince Pie	101

P
Peach Jam	102
Pumpkin Pie	101

R
Raspberry Jam	101
Rice Jelly	85

S
Squash Pie	100
Strawberry Jam	101
Spruce Beer	97

T
Tomato Catsup	84—103
Tomato Sauce	103

Puddings.

A
Arrow Root Pudding	99

B
	Page
Boiled Indian Pudding	85
Bird's Nest Pudding	86

C
Christmas Plum Pudding	105

D
Damson Pudding	99

I
Indian Fruit Pudding	100

O
Orange Pudding	86

P
Plum Pudding	105

R
Rice Pudding, Baked or boiled	100
Rich Apple Pudding	100

S
Sago Pudding	99
Sauce for Pudding	86

T
Tapioca Pudding	99

Meats, Fish, Gravies, &c.

B
Boiled Beef	90
Beef Balls	75
Beef, Cold Tenderloin	76
Beef, Cold Steaks to warm	77
Beef, Minced	77
Beef Steaks broiled	76
Boiled Ham	91
Boiled Salmon	109
Bread Sauce	103
Broiled Cod	110
Broiled Ham	91
Broiled Salmon	109
Broiled Salmon Dried	109

C
Cabbage Soup	106
Caper Sauce	103

CONTENTS.

	Page.
Chicken—good way to prepare	88
Chicken Pie	79
Chicken Pot Pie	91
Chicken Salid	105
Chicken Soup	108
Chicken Soup, No. 2	108
Chowder—how to make	89
Codfish, salt, Stewed	110
Codfish, Salt	110
Cod, or other Fish, to Fry	111
Codfish Cakes	111
Cold Boiled Cod—to make a dish	111
Cold Slaw	88

D
Dried Codfish	110
Dried Cod—a small dish	111
Dried Salmon	109

E
Egg Sauce	102

F
Fried Cod	89—110
Fresh Mackerel Soused	111
Fried Sausages	92
Fried Shad	111

H
Haddock	111

L
Lobster Soup	106

M
Mackerel Salt	112
Melted Butter	102
Minced Meat	90
Mock Turtle Soup	108
Mutton Broth	105
Mutton—to boil Leg of	93
Mutton Chops	77
Mutton, to Stew shoulder of	77

O
Oyster Mouth Soup	106
Oysters—to Fry	89

	Page.
Oyster Sauce	103

P
Parsley & Butter	102
Pig—to Roast	92
Pork Steak	92

R
Roast Pork	90

S
Sandwiches	104
Sausage Meat	92
Sausages	78
Sweet Bread, Liver and Heart	78
Salmon	109
Salmon—to Broil	88
Savoy Soup	106
Shad—to Broil	89
Shad	111
Shell Fish	87
Spare Rib	91
Stewed Lobsters	90
Stewed Oysters	90
Stock for Gravy Soup or Soup	108

T
Turtle Soup	105
Tripe	79

W
White Sauce for Boiled Fowl	103

Vegetables, &c.

Cabbage	93
Coffee—how to Make	101

G
Green Peas	94

M
Mashed Potatoes	93

O
Onions	93

P
Potatoes—to Boil	93

T
Turnips	93

CONTENTS.

COOKERY FOR THE SICK.

	Page.		Page
Broth, Calves' Foot	. 114	Broth, very nourishing	
Broth, Chicken .	. 114	of Veal . .	. 113
Broth, of Beef, Mutton		Jelly Arrowroot .	. 114
and Veal. .	. 113	Jelly Tapioca .	. 114
Broth, quick made	. 113	Tea, Beef . .	. 114

THE LADY'S WORK-BOX.

	Page.		Page.
Bend Work .	. 129	Sofa Pillows .	. 127
Berlin Stitch .	. 128	Settees . .	. 127
Cross Stitch .	. 127	Slippers . .	. 127
Czar Stitch . .	. 128	Straight Cross Stitch	. 127
Fire Side Caps .	. 129	Tent Stitch . .	. 127
Gothic Chairs .	. 129	To dress a frame for	
Irish Stitch . .	. 128	cross Stitch .	. 126
Josephine Stitch .	. 128	To dress a frame for	
Materials for working	. 127	cloth work .	. 127
Pavilion Stitch .	. 127	Weight Cushions.	. 129
Perforated Card .	. 128	Windsor Stitch .	. 127
Rug Bordering .	. 129	Wire Baskets .	. 129

MISCELLANEOUS RECIPES.

	Page.		Page.
Apples, Preserved	. 136	Keep out Red Ants	: 135
Blacking, to make	. 135	Oysters, to Pickle	. 136
Britannia, Water to		Take Ink from Floors	. 136
clean . .	. 135		
Cucumbers, to Pickle	. 136	Washing, Recipe—	
Ice Cream . .	. 135	celebrated .	. 129

DIRECTIONS FOR COLORING GARMENTS, &c.

	Page.		Page.
Carpets, to Clean.	. 134	Green . .	. 132
Clean Silk Goods.	. 134	Light Blue . .	. 132
Discharging Colors	. 132	Red, Crimson, &c.	. 133
Gloves, to Clean	. 134	Brown, inclining to Mul-	
SILKS, TO DYE.		berry . .	. 133
Black, common Mate-		Re-Dying, or changing	
rials . .	. 133	to Color . .	. 129

ETIQUETTE FOR LADIES AND GENTLEMEN.

	PAGE
Behavior in the Street,	117
Behavior at Dinner,	119
Conversation,	120
Dress,	115
General Rules of Behavior,	121
Introductions,	118
Remarks on Habits,	122
The Person,	115
Visiting,	117

LADIES' TOILETTE TABLE.

	PAGE
Dress,	124
Evening Dresses,	124
Flounces,	124
High-necked Dresses,	124
Lotion for Promoting the Growth of Hair, and Preventing it from Turning Grey,	123
Style of Bonnet,	124
Short Cloak,	124
To prevent Loosening of the Hair,	123
To cure Ringworm,	123

CANARY BIRDS.

	PAGE
General Directions,	125
How to Distinguish the Male from the Female,	125
Letter Writer,	125

LADIES DOMESTIC ECONOMY,

AND HOUSEKEEPERS GUIDE.

Rich Small Cake.

Three eggs; three table-spoonfuls of butter, ditto of sugar; three cups of flour; one tea-spoonful of essence of lemon, and half a nutmeg; work these together, roll it thin, cut it in small cakes and bake.

Doughnuts.

Take one pound of flour; a quarter of a pound of butter; three quarters of a pound of brown sugar, rolled fine; one nutmeg, grated; one tea-spoonful of ground cinnamon; one table-spoonful of brewer's yeast; make it into a dough with warm milk; sprinkle flour over it, and cover it with a cloth; set it in a warm place to rise, for one hour or more. When light, roll it out to half an inch thickness; cut it in squares or diamonds. Have a small iron kettle half filled with lard; let it be boiling hot. Drop in a bit of the dough to try it; if it is a fine color, drop in two or three of the cakes at once; keep the kettle in motion all the time the cakes are in, else the lard will burn; when the cakes are a fine color, take them out with a skimmer, and lay them on a sieve to drain.

Beef Balls.

Mince very finely a piece of tender beef, fat and lean; mince an onion, with some parsley; add grated bread crumbs, and season with pepper, salt, grated nutmeg, and lemon-peel; mix all together, and moisten it with an egg beaten; roll it into balls; flour and fry them in boiling fresh dripping, Serve them with fried bread crumbs, or with a thickened brown gravy.

Beef Steaks broiled.

The inside of the sirloin is the best steak—but all are cooked in the same manner. Cut them about half an inch thick—do not beat them; it breaks the cells in which the gravy of the meat is contained and renders it drier and more tasteless.

Have the gridiron hot and the bars rubbed with suet—the fire clear and brisk; sprinkle a little salt over the fire, lay on the steaks, and turn them often. Keep a dish close to the fire, into which you must drain the gravy from the top of the steak as you lift it to turn. The gridiron should be set in a slanting direction on the coals, to prevent the fat from dropping into the fire and making a smoke. But should a smoke occur, take off the gridiron a moment, till it is over. With a good fire of coals, steaks will be thoroughly done in fifteen minutes. These are much healthier for delicate stomachs than *rare done steaks.*

When done lay them in a hot plate, put a small slice of good butter on each piece—sprinkle *a little* salt, pour the gravy from the dish by the fire and serve them hot as possible. Pickles and finely scraped horse-radish are served with them.

I have now given the most important recipes for cooking beef.—The re-cooking requires skill and judgment which experience only can give. When well done it makes excellent dishes, and is economical in housekeeping. The following are good recipes.

Beef, cold Tenderloin.

Cut off entire the inside of a large sirloin of beef, brown it all over in a stewpan, and then add a quart of water, two table-spoonfuls of vinegar, some pepper, salt, ane a large onion finely minced; cover the pan closely, and let it stew till the beef be very tender. Garnish with pickles.

Beef Minced.

Mince your beef very small ; put it into a saucepan with a little gravy and a little of the fat of fowl or any other fat, season according to your taste, then let it simmer over a gentle fire till it is sufficiently done.

Boiled beef, when thoroughly done, is excellent to eat cold, as a relish at breakfast. The slices should be cut even and very thin.

Beef, cold Steaks to warm.

Lay them in a stewpan, with one large onion cut in quarters, six berries of allspice, the same of black pepper, cover the steaks with boiling water, let them stew gently one hour, thicken the liquor with flour and butter rubbed together on a plate ; if a pint of gravy, about one ounce of flour, and the like weight of butter, will do ; put it into the stewpan, shake it well over the fire for five minutes, and it is ready; lay the steaks and onions on a dish and pour the gravy through a seive over them.

Mutton Chops.

Cut the chops off a loin or the best end of a neck of mutton; pare off the fat, dip them in a beaten egg and strew over them grated bread, seasoned with salt nd finely minced parsley—then fry them in a little butter, and make a gravy, or broil them over coals and butter them, in a hot dish. Garnish with fried parsley.

To Stew a shoulder of Mutton.

Bone and flatten a shoulder of mutton, sprinkle over it pepper and salt, roll it up tightly, bind it with tape, and put it into a stewpan that will just hold it, pour over it a well seasoned gravy made with the bones, cover the pan closely, and let it stew till tender; before serving take off the tape, thicken the gravy. It will take about three hours to stew the shoulders.

Sweet Bread, Liver, and Heart.

A very good way to cook the sweet bread is to fry three or four slices of pork till brown, then take them up and put in the sweet bread, and fry it over a moderate fire. When you have taken up the sweet bread, mix a couple of teaspoonfuls of flour with a little water and stir it into the fat—let it boil, then turn it over the sweet bread. Another way is to parboil them, and let them get cold, then, cut them in pieces about an inch thick, dip them in the yolk of an egg, and fine bread crumbs, sprinkle salt, pepper, and sage on them before dipping them in the egg, fry them a light brown. Make a gravy after you have taken them up, by stirring a little flour and water mixed smooth into the fat, add spices and wine if you like. The liver and heart are good cooked in the same manner, or broiled.

Sausages.

Chop fresh pork very fine, the lean and fat together, (there should be rather more of the lean than the fat,) season it highly with salt, pepper, sage, and other sweet herbs, if you like them—a little saltpetre tends to preserve them. To tell whether they are seasoned enough, do up a little into a cake, and fry it. If not seasoned enough, add more seasoning, and fill your skins, which should be previously cleaned thoroughly. A little flour mixed with the meat tends to prevent the fat from running out when cooked. Sausage-meat is good, done up in small cakes and fried. In summer when fresh pork cannot be procured, very good sausage-cakes may be made of raw beef, chopped fine with salt pork, and seasoned with pepper and sage. When sausages are fried, they should not be pricked, and they will cook nicer, to have a little fat put with them.

They should be cooked slowly. If you do not like them very fat, take them out of the pan when nearly done, and finish cooking them on a gridiron. Bologna sausages are made of equal weight each, of ham, veal, and pork, chopped very fine, seasoned high, and boiled in casings, till tender, then dried.

Tripe.

After being scoured, should be soaked in salt and water seven or eight days, changing the water every other day, then boil it till tender, which will take eight or ten hours. It is then fit for broiling, frying, or pickling. It is pickled in the same manner as souse.

Curries.

Chickens, pigeons, mutton chops, lobsters and veal, all make good curries. If the curry dish is to be made of fowls, they should be jointed. Boil the meat till tender, in just sufficient water to cover it, and add a little salt. Just before the meat is boiled enough to take up, fry three or four slices of pork till brown—take them up, and put in the chickens. Let them brown, then add part of the liquor in which they were boiled, one or two tea-spoonfuls of curry powder, and the fried pork. Mix a tea-spoonful of curry powder with a tea cup of boiled rice, or a little flour and water mixed—turn it on to the curry, and let it stew a few minutes.

Chicken Pie.

Joint the chickens, which should be young and tender—boil them in just sufficient water to cover them. When nearly tender, take them out of the liquor, and lay them in a deep pudding dish, lined with pie crust. To each layer of chicken, put three or four slices of pork—add a little of the liquor in which they were boiled, and a couple of ounces of butter, cut into small pieces—sprinkle a little flour over the whole, cover it with nice pie crust, and ornament the top with some of your pastry. Bake it in a quick oven one hour.

Curry Powder.

Mix an ounce of ginger, one of mustard, one of pepper, three of coriander seed, the same quantity of turmeric, a quarter of an ounce of cayenne pepper, half an ounce of cardamums, and the same of cummin seed and cinnamon. Pound the whole fine, sift and keep it in a bottle corked tight.

Green Corn Cake.

Mix a pint of grated green corn with three table-spoonfuls of milk, a tea-cup of flour, half a tea-cup of melted butter, one egg, a tea-spoonful of salt, and half a tea-spoonful of pepper. Drop this mixture into hot butter by the spoonful, let the cakes fry eight or ten minutes. These cakes are nice served up with meat for dinner.

Muffins.

Mix a quart of wheat flour smoothly with a pint and a half of luke-warm milk, half a tea-cup of yeast, a couple of beaten eggs, a heaping tea-spoonful of salt, and a couple of table-spoonfuls of luke-warm melted butter. Set the batter in a warm place to rise. When light, butter your muffin cups, turn in the mixture and bake the muffins till a light brown.

Molasses Dough Cake.

Melt half a tea-cup of butter, mix it with a tea-cup of molasses, the juice and chopped rind of a fresh lemon, a tea-spoonful of cinnamon—work the whole with the hand into three tea-cups of raised dough, together with a couple of beaten eggs. Work it with the hand for ten or twelve minutes, then put it into buttered pans. Let it remain ten or fifteen minutes before baking it.

Rice Waffles.

Take a tea-cup and a half of boiled rice—warm it with a pint of milk, mix it smooth, then take it from the fire, stir in a pint of cold milk, and a tea-spoonful of salt. Beat four eggs, and stir them in, together with sufficient flour to make it a thick batter.

Savoy Cakes.

Beat eight eggs to a froth—the whites and yolks should be beaten separately, then mixed together, and a pound of powdered white sugar stirred in gradually. Beat the whole well together, for eight or ten minutes, then add the grated rind of a fresh lemon, and half the juice, a couple of table-spoonfuls of coriander seed. Drop this mixture by the large spoonful on two buttered baking plates, several inches apart, sift white sugar over them, and bake them immediately in a quick, but not a furiously hot oven.

Lemon Pie.

For one pie, take a couple of good sized fresh lemons, squeeze out the juice, and mix it with half a pint of molasses, or sufficient sugar to make the juice sweet. Chop the peel fine, line deep pie plates with your pastry, then sprinkle on a layer of your chopped lemon peel, turn in part of the mixed sugar or molasses and juice, then cover the whole with pie crust, rolled very thin—put in another layer of peel, sweetened juice, and crust, and so, till all the lemon is used. Cover the whole with a thick crust, and bake the pie about half an hour.

Dyspepsia Bread.

Three quarts of unbolted wheat meal; 1 quart of soft warm water; a gill of fresh yeast, a gill of molasses, 1 tea-spoonful of saleratus. This will make 2 loaves, and should remain in the oven at least 2 hours. It will need fron 8 to 12 hours to rise.

A Light Cake, to be Baked in Cups.

Take a pint bowl full and a half of sugar, one and a half cups of butter rubbed in two pint bowls of flour, two cups of sour cream, a tea-spoonful of salæratus, table-spoonful of rose water, four eggs well beaten, and a little nutmeg.

Composition Cake.

Take four cups of flour, four of sugar, two cups of butter, five eggs, half pint of cream, tea-spoonful of salæratus, spice to suit your taste. Beat all well together, and bake in a butter tin or in cups.

Indian Griddle Cakes.

Take one pint of Indian meal and one cup of flour, a little salt and ginger, a table-spoonful of molasses, a tea-spoonful of salæratus, sour milk enough to make a stiff batter. Bake them on a griddle like buckwheat cakes.

Common Plumb Cake.

Mix five cups of butter with ten cups of flour, five cups of sugar, add six cups stoned raisins, a little cinnamon and mace finely powdered, half a cup of good yeast put into a pint of new milk, warm and mix the dough, let it stand till it is light.

Pound Cake.

One pound dried sifted flour, the same of loaf sugar, and the whites of twelve eggs and the yolks of seven. Beat the butter to a cream, add the sugar by degrees, then the eggs and flour; beat it all well together for an hour, mixing a table-spoonful of rose-water, a little nutmeg or cinnamon, two cups of cream, and a tea-spoonful of salæratus. To be baked in a quick oven.

Tea Cake.

A quart of flour, one pint of sour cream, tea-spoonful salæratus, two cups of molasses, a little cinnamon and salt, make a stiff paste, and bake in a moderate oven.

Breakfast Butter Cakes.

One quart of sour milk, one tea-spoonful salæratus, a little salt, one and a half cups boiled rice, two tablespoonfuls molasses or half cup sugar, a little ginger, and flour enough to make a stiff batter.

Buck-Wheat Cakes.

Take one quart of buck-wheat meal, half a cup of new yeast, a tea-spoonful of salæratus, a little salt and sufficient new milk or cold water to make a thick batter. Put it in a warm place to rise. When it has risen sufficiently, bake it on a griddle or in a spider. The griddle must be well buttered, and the cakes are better to be small and thin.

Plain Indian Cakes.

Take a quart of sifted Indian meal, sprinkle a little salt over it, mix it with scalding water, stirring it well; bake on a tin in a stove oven. Indian Cake is made with butter-milk, or sour milk, with a little cream or butter rubbed into the meal, and a tea-spoonful of salæratus.

Butter Cakes for Tea.

Beat two eggs, put them in half pint of milk, and a tea-cup of cream, with half a tea-spoonful of salæratus dissolved in the cream, a little salt, cinnamon and a little rose-water if you like, stir in sifted flour till the batter is smooth and thick. Bake them on a griddle or in a pan. Butter the pan well, drop the batter in small round cakes and quite thin. They must be turned and nicely browned. Lay them on a plate, in a pile, with a little butter between each layer.

Cream Cakes.

In the country where cream is plenty, this is a favorite cake at the tea-table. One quart of flour, one pint of cream, a little sour cream, one tea-spoonful of salæratus dissolved in the sour cream. If the flour is not made sufficiently wet with the above quantity of cream, add more sweet cream.

Tomato Sauce.

Peel and slice twelve tomatoes, picking out the seeds—add three powdered crackers, pepper and salt to your taste; stew twenty minutes.

Rolls.

Rub into a pound of flour half a tea-cup full of butter; add half a tea-cup of sweet yeast, a little salt, and sufficient warm milk to make a stiff dough, cover and put it where it will be kept warm, and it will rise in two hours. Then make into rolls or round cakes. They will bake in a quick oven in fifteen minutes.

Dyspepsia Cake.

Take five cups of flour, two of sugar, two cups of milk, a little salt, and one tea-spoonful of salæratus.

Indian Cake.

Take three cups of Indian meal, two cups of flour, one half a tea-cup of molasses, a little salt, one teaspoonful of salæratus, and mix them with cold water.

Hard Wafers.

Take half a pound of butter, half a pound of sugar, three eggs, one table-spoonful of cinnamon, two-tablespoonsful of rose water, and flour enough to make it a thick dough.

Blanc-Mange.

Take half an ounce of Iceland moss, and one quart of new milk. Simmer them together until they become a jelly. Add half a tea-cup of rose water, let them scald half an hour and strain.

Loaf Cake.

Two pounds of flour, half a pound of sugar, quarter of butter, three eggs, one gill of milk, half a tea-cup sweet emptyings, cinnamon and rose water.

Ginger-Bread.

Four cups of flour, three eggs, one cup of butter, two of sugar, one of cream, ginger, nutmeg, salæratus.

Arrow-root Custards.

Four eggs, one dessert spoonful of arrow-root, one pint of milk sweetened, and spiced to the taste.

Rice Jelley.

Boil one-fourth pound of rice flour with half a pound of loaf sugar in one quart of water, until the whole becomes one glutinous mass. Then strain off the jelly and let it stand to cool.

Measure Cake.

One cup of cream, one of sugar, two and a half of flour, two eggs, a tea-spoonful of salæratus, nutmeg.

Boiled Indian Pudding.

One quart of sour milk, a tea-spoonful of salæratus half a cup of molasses, a tea-cupful of chopped suet meal enough to make it stiff.

Best Cup Cake.

Five cups of flour, three of sugar, one of milk, three eggs, one tea-spoonful of salæratus, raisens, one cup of butter, nutmeg, rose-water.

Icing for Cake.

Four pounds of loaf sugar, the whites of nineteen eggs, one table-spoonful of starch, half ounce gum-arabic, table-spoonful rose-water.

Seed Cakes.

Four cups of flour, one and a half of cream or milk, half of butter, three eggs, half a cup of seeds, two cups of sugar, a tea-spoonful of salæratus, and rose-water.

Sugar Ginger-Bread.

Take two pounds of flour, one of butter and one of sugar, five eggs well beaten, two ounces of powdered ginger, and a tea-spoonful of salæratus, with nutmeg and rose-water.

Bakers' Ginger-Bread.

Three-fourths of a pound of flour, one cup of molasses, one-fourth of butter, one ounce of salæratus, and one of ginger.

Symballs.

Four cups of flour, a cup and a half of sugar, half a cup of butter, three eggs, a cup of sour cream, a tea-spoonful of salæratus, a little nutmeg, ginger, salt, and a tea-spoonful of rose-water.

Cream Cake.

One pound of flour, one pound of sugar, half a pound of butter, half a pint of cream, four eggs, one pound of currants, a tea-spoonful of salæratus, a table-spoonful of rose-water, or a glass of brandy; spice for your taste.

Orange Pudding.

Four oranges, eight ounces of butter, eight ounces of sugar, and eight eggs.

Bird's-nest Pudding.

Put into three pints of boiling milk six crackers pounded fine and one pint of raisins; when cool add four eggs well beaten, a little sugar, and five good sized apples pared, with the core carefully removed. To be eaten with warm sauce.

Pudding Sauce.

One pint of sugar, a table-spoonful of vinegar, a piece of butter the size of an egg boiled fifteen minutes: add a table-spoonful of rose-water and a little nutmeg: boil with the sugar, in nearly a pint of water, a large table-spoonful of flour.

Conserve Roses.

Bruise the leaves of red roses in a mortar; to every pound add a pound of sugar; mix the sugar well with the roses in alternate layers; pack it light in an earthen vessel, and cover it from the air.

To Preserve Barberries.

To one pound of the berries add one pound of sugar,

a pint and a half of molasses; and simmer them together half an hour or more, until they become soft.

To Make Good Yeast.

Take as many hops as you can hold in your hand twice, put them into three pints of cold water; put them over the fire, and let them boil twenty minutes: then strain the water into an earthen or stone jar, and stir in while the water is scalding hot, flour enough to make a stiff batter: let it stand till about milk-warm; then add a tea-cupful of old yeast to make it rise, and a tea-spoonful of salæratus dissolved in the old yeast; stir it well and put the jar in a warm place to rise. Some add Indian meal enough (after it has risen well) to make it into cakes and dry it on a board in the sun. This is very convenient, especially in hot weather,—a small cake soaked in a little warm water is enough to make a large pan of dough rise.

Milk Yeast.

One pint of new milk, one tea-spoonful of fine salt, and a large spoonful of flour; stir these well together, set the mixture by the fire, and keep it just lukewarm —it will be fit for use in an hour. Twice the quantity of common yeast is necessary: it will not keep long. Bread made of this yeast dries very soon; but in summer it is sometimes convenient to make this kind when yeast is needed suddenly.

Yeast should not be kept in a tin vessel. If you find the old yeast sour, and have not time to prepare new, put in salæratus, a tea-spoonful to a pint of yeast, when ready to use it. If it foams up lively, it will raise the bread; if it does not, never use it.

Shell Fish.

Oysters and clams generally agree well with those who like them; but lobsters should be eaten cautiously, as they are very hard to digest.

Calf's-Foot Jelly.

Boil four feet, nicely cleaned, in a gallon of water till reduced to one quart; strain it, and when cool

take off the top. In taking out the jelly avoid the
settlings. Add a half-pound of sugar, the juice of two
lemons, and, if you please, the whites of four eggs to
make it clear: boil all together a few minutes, and
strain it through a cloth.

Currant Jelly.

Place a jar of currants in a kettle of boiling water
till the currants become wilted; then squeeze them
through a cloth. Add a pint of sugar to a pint of
juice; boil it slowly till it becomes ropy. It should
be frequently stirred and skimmed while simmering.

Black Currant Jelly.

Make in the same way. Good for a sore throat.

To Broil Salmon.

Cut in slices an inch or an inch and a half thick, dry
it in a clean cloth, sprinkle over it a little salt, put
your gridiron over good live coals, rub the bars with
a little lard, lay the salmon on with the skin next to
the gridiron, and when done on one side, lay a dish
over the salmon, turn the gridiron over, rub the bars
again with lard; then slip the salmon from the dish
on to the gridiron. In that way you will not break
up the fish by turning it.

A very good Way to Prepare a Chicken.

Wash, and cut the chicken into joints; scald, and
take off the skin; put the pieces in a stew-pan, with
very little parsley, thyme, salt and pepper; add a
quart of water, and a piece of butter the size of an
egg; stew it an hour and a half; take up the chicken,
and if there is no gravy, add another piece of butter,
very little water, and sprinkle in a table-spoonful of
flour, and let it boil ten minutes.

Cold Slaw.

Take off seven or eight outside leaves of a cabbage,
and cut off as much of the stump as can be got off;
then cut the small head in two, wash it well, and cut
it up very fine; put it in a dish with a pint of good
vinegar and a little salt.

To Fry Cod or other Fish.

It is much more difficult to fry fish than meat. Lard or dripping is better than butter, because the latter burns so easily. The fat fried from salt pork is the best of all: the fire must be clear and hot, but not furious; the fat hot when the fish is put in; and there should be sufficient to cover the fish. Skim the fat before laying in the fish. Cut the cod in slices, half or three quarters of an inch thick; rub them with Indian meal to prevent breaking. Fry it thoroughly. Trout and perch are fried in the same manner, only do not rub Indian meal on them. Dip in the white of an egg and bread crumbs, or dust with flour.

To Broil Shad.

This is a very fine, delicious fish. Clean, wash, and split the shad, let it dry a few minutes, put it on the gridiron with the fleshy part up, and put it over good lively coals to cook ten minutes, then turn it in the same way that you do salmon. When it is done, take it up, sprinkle on a little salt and pepper, and lay on two or three pieces of butter to moisten it.

To Make a Chowder.

Cut three or four slices of fat pork; fry them a very little; lay them in the bottom of a stew-kettle. Cut a fresh cod into thin slices; place two slices of fish on the pork; then put in a layer of split crackers; pare and wash eight potatoes, and cut them into thin slices; put on a layer of the sliced potatoes, then alternately the other materials, till the kettle is full; season with pepper and a little salt. Mix one table-spoonful of flour with a tea-cupful of cold water, and pour in after the chowder begins to stew. Put in a quart of water, cover the stew-kettle very tight, and let it stew three hours.

To Fry Oysters.

Make a batter, as for pancakes; put one or two oysters into a spoonful of the batter, and fry them to a light brown. Fry them in hot fat, the same as pancakes.

Stewed Oysters.

Three quarts are enough for a small family dinner. Put them into a stew-pan, with a piece of butter the size of an egg; stew them well ten minutes: toast three or four slices of bread, cut them, lay them in the bottom of a dish, and pour the oysters over them.

Stewed Lobsters.

A middling sized lobster is best; pick all the meat from the shells as whole as possible; put it in a stew-pan with a piece of butter the size of a large egg, a little pepper, salt, and a tea-cupful of weak vinegar: stew about twenty minutes. It should be eaten when very hot.

Boiled Beef.

To have it very tender, it should boil slowly, and the pot be well skimmed. The meat should be well covered with water, so that the skim may be removed easily. When beef is very salt, it should boil three-quarters of an hour: then take it up, throw away the water it has boiled in, fill up the pot with fresh water, replace the beef, and let it boil gently three hours. The *round* is the best piece to boil—then the *H-bone*. Observe to take off all the scum as it rises.

Minced Meat.

Take cold boiled beef, removing all bones and gristle, with a good proportion of cold boiled potatoes; chop them midling fine; fry three slices of salt pork in a spider; when the pork is brown, take it up, and put in the minced meat and potatoes. Let it cook twenty minutes. Take it up in a covered dish, with the slices of pork placed on the top of the dish.

Roast Pork.

Take a leg of pork; one weighing eight pounds will require full three hours and a half to roast. Wash it clean, and dry it with a cloth. Make a stuffing of crackers powdered fine, with half a pint of thick cream, two eggs, a little salt, pepper, sweet marjoram, and summer savory; cook about ten minutes. Put this under the skin of the knuckle, and in deep incisions made in the thick part of the leg.

Do not put it too near the fire; it must be floured, and moistened often with the drippings until it is done; then skim the fat from the gravy, add a little flour, and boil it well a few minutes. Apple-sauce or currant jelly is proper to accompany roasted pork; also, potatoes, mashed squash, turnips and pickles.

Spare Rib.

If large and thick it will require two or three hours to roast. A very thin one may roast in an hour. Lay the thick end to the fire; when you put it down, put into the vessel a pint of water and a table-spoonful of salt. It should be floured, and basted often with the drippings. The shoulder, loin and chine are roasted in the same way. A shoulder is the most economical to buy, and is excellent boiled. Pork is always salted before it is boiled.

Chicken Pot Pie.

Wash and cut the chicken into joints; take out the breast bone; boil them about twenty minutes; take them up, wash out your kettle; fry two or three slices of fat salt pork, and put in the bottom of the kettle; then put in the chicken, with about three pints of water, a piece of butter the size of an egg; sprinkle in a tea-spoonful of pepper, and cover over the top with a light crust. It will require an hour to cook.

Broiled Ham.

Ham should be cut in thin slices, and broiled quick on a gridiron, set over good live coals. If the ham is too salt, soak it in hot water before broiling: if it is necessary to do this, dry it well with a cloth before putting it on the gridiron. Fry what eggs you want in a part good sweet lard, and a part butter; put an egg on each slice of ham.

Boiled Ham.

A ham, if dry, should be soaked twelve hours in warm water. Then put it on in cold water, and let it simmer, and boil five or six hours. It is best when quite cold. Boiled ham is very good to broil.

Fried Sausages.

Sausages are best when quite fresh. Fry two or three slices of fat pork; then put the sausages into the hot fat, pricking them several times with a fork. Fry them over a slow fire till they are a nice brown.

Sausage Meat.

Chop two pounds of lean beef, with one of fat pork, very fine; mix with this three tea-spoonsful of salt, five of powdered sage, five of sweet marjoram, three of black pepper. To make this into small cakes, and fry in the same manner as sausages, is very good for breakfast.

To Roast a Pig.

A pig about three weeks old is the best. It should be killed in the morning, if it is to be eaten for dinner. Make a stuffing with about six powdered crackers, one table-spoonful of sage, two of sweet marjoram, half a pint of cream, two eggs, and a little salt and pepper. Mix these well together, and let it stew about fifteen minutes. Wash the pig in cold water; cut off the petti-toes, leaving the skin long to wrap around the ends of the legs; then fill the belly with the stuffing, and sew it up. The liver and heart should be boiled with five or six pepper corns, and chopped fine for the gravy. When the pig is put down to roast, put in a pint of water, and a table-spoonful of salt: when it begins to roast, flour it well, and baste it with the drippings, and continue to do so until it is done. It requires constant care. A small pig will roast in three hours.

Pork Steak.

Cut them off a neck or loin; broil them over good live coals, turning them frequently: they broil in ten minutes. Sprinkle with salt and pepper when put in the dish, and add a small piece of sweet butter to every piece of steak.

To Boil a Leg of Mutton.

Cut off the shank bone, and trim the knuckle; if it weigh nine pounds it will require three hours to cook it. Parsley and butter, or capen-sauce should be served with it—onion-sauce, turnips, spinage and potatoes are all good.

To Boil Potatoes.

Pare, wash, and throw them into a pan of cold water: then put them on to boil in a clean pot with cold water sufficient to cover them, and sprinkle over a little salt; then let them boil slowly, uncovered, till you can pass a fork through them; pour off the water, and put them where they will keep hot till wanted. When done in this way they will be very mealy and dry. Potatoes, either boiled or roasted, should *never be covered* to keep them hot.

Mashed Potatoes.

When old, potatoes are best boiled and mashed, with a little butter, salt and cream, or milk; they may be also sliced, and fried raw, in hot salt pork fat, or after they are boiled. Both these dishes are relished. But a plain boiled or roasted potato, when well cooked, is the best and most wholesome; and although not a substitute for bread, is one of the most useful vegetable productions.

Turnips.

Should be pared, put into water with a little salt, and boiled till tender; then squeeze them thoroughly from the water, mash them smooth, and add a piece of butter and a little pepper and salt.

Cabbage

Requires to be well washed before it is cooked; boil it in a large quantity of water, with a little salt, till it is soft and tender; skim the water carefully when it first boils. If the head is large, cut it; but a small head is best.

Onions.

Peel and put them into boiling milk and water,—

(water alone will do, but it is not so good.) When tender, take them up, and salt them, and turn a little melted butter over them.

Green Peas

Should be young and fresh shelled; wash them clean; put them into a bag, and that into plenty of boiling water, with a little salt, and a tea-spoonful of pounded loaf sugar; boil them till tender. Green peas are a most delicious vegetable when cooked enough—half done, they are hard and very unwholesome. It takes from half an hour to an hour to boil them. Never let them stand in the water after they are done. Season them with a little butter and salt.

Lemon Cake.

Take one tea-cup of butter, and three of powdered loaf sugar; rub them to a cream; stir into them the yolks of five eggs well beaten; dissolve a tea-spoonful of salæratus in a tea-cup of milk, and add the milk; add the juice and grated peel of one lemon, and the hites of five eggs; and sift in, as light as possible, our tea-cups of flour. Bake in two long tins about half an hour. It is much improved by icing.

New-York Cup Cake.

Take four eggs, four tumblers of sifted flour, three mblers of powdered white sugar, one tumbler of butr, one tumbler of rich milk, one glass of white wine, a grated nutmeg, a tea-spoonful of powdered cinnaron, and a small tea-spoonful of salæratus. Warm the milk and put in the butter, keeping it by the fire till the butter is melted; stir into the milk the eggs beaten very light, in turn with the flour; and the spice and wine; and, lastly, the salæratus dissolved in a little vinegar: stir all very hard; butter small tin pans, half fill them, and bake in a moderate oven of equal heat throughout.

Cake without Eggs.

T te one cup of butter, three of sugar, one pint of sour ilk or cream, a pint and a half or two pints of flour, one pound of raisins, a spoonful of salæratus, and spice to your taste. Mix the ingredients properly prepared, and bake about an hour.

Good Family Cake.

Take two pounds of flour, half a pound of butter half of white sugar, one pint of milk, three eggs, one gill of yeast, half a spoonful of mace, or other spice, to your taste. Mix well, half your flour with the yeast and milk, and let it stand till perfectly light. Add the butter, eggs, sugar, and spice together, and stir in the remainder of your flour; then gently pour this to the first mixture; let all stand till perfectly light; then bake it in pans.

Jelly Cake.

Take six ounces of butter and eight of sugar, and rub them to a cream; stir into it eight well beaten eggs and a pound of sifted flour; add the grated rind and juice of a fresh lemon, and turn the mixture on scolloped tin plates that have been well buttered. The cakes should not be more than a quarter of an inch thick on the plates. Bake them immediately, in a quick oven, till of a light brown. Pile them on a plate, with a layer of jelly or marmalade on the top of each.

Ginger Nuts.

Take one quart of molasses; mix with it one pound and three-quarters of sugar, one and a quarter of butter, seven of flour, four ounces of ginger, a nutmeg, and a little cinnamon.

Ginger Snaps.

Take one pint of molasses, one tea-cup of butter, one spoonful of ginger, and one tea-spoonful of salæratus; and boil all the ingredients thoroughly; when nearly cold, add as much flour as can be rolled into the mixture.

Jumbles.

Rub to a cream a pound of sugar, and half a pound of butter; add eight well beaten eggs, essence of lemon or rose-water to the taste, and flour to make the jumbles stiff enough for rolling out. Roll out, in powdered sugar, about half an inch wide and four inches long, and form them into rings by joining the ends. Lay them on flat buttered tins, and bake in a quick oven.

Rich Jumbles.

Rub to a cream a pound of butter and a pound of sugar; mix with it a pound and a half of flour, four eggs, and very little brandy. Roll the cakes in powdered sugar, and bake.

Hoe Cakes.

Scald a quart of Indian meal with just sufficient water to make a thick batter; stir in two spoonsful of butter, and two tea-spoonsful of salt. Turn it into a buttered cake pan, bake about half an hour.

Indian Corn Cakes.

Mix a quart of Indian meal with a handful of wheat flour, stir in a quart of warmed milk, a tea-spoonful of salt, and two spoonsful of yeast; stir alternately into the milk, the meal and three well-beaten eggs; when light, bake as buckwheat cakes, on a griddle; send them to the table hot. Should the batter sour, stir in a little salæratus dissolved in luke-warm water, letting it set half an hour before baking.

Apple Snow.

Put twelve good tart apples in cold water, and set them over a slow fire; when soft, drain off the water, strip the skins off the apples, core them, and lay them in a deep dish. Beat the whites of twelve eggs to a stiff froth; put half a pound of powdered white sugar to the apples, beat them to a stiff froth, and add the beaten eggs. Beat the whole to a stiff snow, then turn it into a dessert dish, and ornament it with myrtle or box.

Yeast of Cream of Tartar and Salæratus.

Heat your oven; mix two tea-spoonsful of cream of tartar with one quart of flour; then dissolve one tea-spoonful of salæratus in warm water, and mix it with

the flour, adding water enough to make a soft dough.
As soon as thoroughly kneaded, place it in your oven
until sufficiently baked, and the bread will be tender
and of the nicest kind. Biscuit may be made in the
same way by adding a little shortning.

Spruce Beer.

Allow an ounce of hops and a spoonful of ginger to
a gallon of water. When well boiled, strain it, and
put in a pint of molasses and half an ounce or less of
the essence of spruce: when cool, add a tea-cup of
yeast, put it into a clean tight cask, and let it ferment
for a day or two: then bottle it for use.

Brown or Dyspepsia Bread.

This bread is now best known as "Graham Bread,"
—not that Doctor Graham invented or discovered the
manner of its preparation, but that he has been un-
wearied and successful in recommending it to the pub
lic. It is an excellent article of diet for the dyspeptic,
and the costive; and for most persons of sedentary
habits it would be beneficial. It agrees well with
children; and, in short, I think it should be used in
every family, though not to the exclusion of fine bread.
The most difficult point in manufacturing this bread
is to obtain good pure meal. It is said that much of
the bread commonly sold as *dyspepsia* is made of the
bran or middlings, from which the fine flour has been
separated; and that *saw-dust* is sometimes mixed with
the meal. To be certain that it is good, send good clean
wheat to the mill, have it ground rather coarsely, and
keep the meal in a dry cool place. Before using it,
sift it through a common hair-seive; this will separate the very coarse and harsh particles.

Take six quarts of this wheat meal, one tea-cupful
of good yeast, and half a tea-cup of molasses; mix
these with a pint of milk-warm water and a tea-spoonful of perlash or salæratus. Make a hole in the flour,
and stir this mixture in the middle of the meal till it
is like batter. Then proceed as with fine flour bread.
Make the dough when sufficiently light into four
loaves, which will weigh two pounds per loaf when

baked. It requires a hotter oven than fine flour bread, and must bake about an hour and a half.

Rye and Indian Bread.

This is a sweet and nourishing diet, and generally acceptable to children.

It is economical, and when wheat is scarce, is a pretty good substitute for dyspepsia bread.

There are many different proportions of mixing it; some put one-third Indian meal with two of rye; others like one-third rye and two of Indian; others prefer it half and half.

If you use the largest proportion of rye meal, make your dough stiff, so that it will mould into loaves; when it is two-thirds Indian, it should be softer and baked in deep earthen or tin pans after the following rules:

Take *four quarts* of sifted Indian meal; put it into a glazed earthen pan, sprinkle over it a table-spoonful of fine salt; pour over it about two quarts of boiling water, stir and work it till every part of the meal is thoroughly wet; Indian absorbs a greater quantity of water. When it is about milk warm, work in two quarts of rye meal, half a pint of lively yeast, mixed with a pint of warm water; add more warm water if needed. Work the mixture well with your hands; it should be stiff, but not as firm as flour dough. Have ready a large, deep, well buttered pan; put in the dough, and smooth the top by putting your hand in warm water, and then patting down the loaf. Set this to rise in a warm place in the winter; in the summer it should not be put by the fire. When it begins to crack on the top, which will usually be in about an hour or an hour and a half, put it into a well-heated oven, and bake it three or four hours. It is better to let it stand in the oven all night, unless the weather is warm. Indian meal requires to be well cooked. The loaf will weigh between seven and eight pounds. Pan bread keeps best in large loaves.

Many use milk in mixing bread; in the country, where milk is plentiful, it is a good practice, as bread is certainly richer wet with sweet milk than with water; but it will not keep so long in warm weather.

Baking can very well be done in a stove; during the winter this is an economical way of cooking—but the stove must be carefully watched, or there is danger of scorching the bread.

Arrow-root Pudding.

From a quart of new milk take a small tea-cupful, and mix it with two large spoonsful of arrow-root. Boil the remainder of the milk, and stir it amongst the arrow-root;—add, when nearly cold, four well beaten eggs, with two ounces of powdered loaf sugar, and the same of fresh butter broken into small bits; season with grated nutmeg. Mix it well together, and bake it in a buttered dish fifteen or twenty minutes.

Damson Pudding.

Make a batter with three well beaten eggs, a pint of milk and of flour and brown sugar four table-spoonsful each;—stone a pint of damsons, and mix them with the batter; boil it in a buttered basin for an hour and a half.

Sago Pudding.

Boil five table-spoonsful of sago, well picked and washed in a quart of milk till quite soft, with a stick of cinnamon. Then stir in one tea-cup of butter and two of powdered loaf sugar. When it is cold add six eggs well beaten, and a little grated nutmeg. Mix all well together, and bake it in a buttered dish about three-quarters of an hour. Brown sugar, if dried, will answer very well to sweeten it.

Tapioca Pudding.

Wash four large table-spoonsful of tapioca, and soak it for an hour in a little warm water; strain it through a seive, and mix it with the well beaten yolks of four, and the whites of two eggs, a quart of good milk, half a tea-spoonful of grated nutmeg, and sweeten it with sugar. Bake it in a dish, with or without puff paste round the edges, one hour.

Rice Pudding, Baked or Boiled.

Wash in cold water and pick very clean six ounces of rice; boil it in one quart of milk, with a bit of cinnamon, very gently, till it is quite tender; it will take about an hour; be careful to stir it often. Take it from the fire, pick out the cinnamon, and stir in a teacupful of sugar, half a cup of butter, three eggs well beaten, a little powdered nutmeg—stir it till it is quite smooth. You can line a pie-dish with puff paste, or bake it in a buttered dish, which is better; three-quarters of an hour will bake it.

If you wish it more like custard, add one more egg and half a pint of milk.

If you boil it you can add whatever fruit you like; three ounces of currants, or raisins, or apples minced fine; it will take an hour to boil it.

Serve with wine sauce or butter and sugar.

Rich Apple Pudding.

Peel and core six very large apples, stew them in six table-spoonsful of water, with the rind of a lemon; when soft, beat them to a pulp, add six ounces of good brown sugar, six well beaten eggs, a pint of rich cream, and a tea-spoonful of lemon juice; line a dish with a puff paste, and when baked, stick all over the top thin chips of candied citron and lemon-peel.

Indian Fruit Pudding.

Take a pint of hot milk, and stir in sifted Indian meal till the batter is stiff; add a tea-spoonful of salt and a little molasses; then stir in a pint of whortleberries, or chopped sweet apple. Tie it in a cloth that has been wet, and leave room for it to swell, or put it in a pudding-pan, and tie a cloth over—boil three hours. The water must boil when it is put in. You can use cranberries, and use sweet sauce.

Squash Pie.

Pare, take out the seeds, and stew the squash till very soft and dry. Strain or rub it through a seive or colander. Mix this with good milk till it is as thick as batter; sweeten it with sugar. Allow five eggs to a quart of milk, beat the eggs well, add them to the squash, and season with rose-water, cinnamon, nutmeg, or whatever spices you like. Line a pie-plate with crust, fill and bake about an hour.

Pumpkin Pie.

Stew the pumpkin dry, and make it like squash pie, only season rather higher. In the country, where this real yankee pie is prepared in perfection, ginger is almost always used with other spices. There, too, part cream instead of milk is mixed with the pumpkin, which gives it a richer flavor.

Roll the paste rather thicker than for fruit pies, as there is but one crust. If the pie is large and deep, it will require to bake an hour in a brisk oven.

Family Mince Pies.

Boil three pounds of lean beef till tender, and when cold chop it fine. Chop three pounds of clear beef suet, and mix the meat, sprinkling in a table-spoonful of salt.

Pare, core and chop fine six pounds of good apples; stone four pounds of raisins, and chop them; wash and dry two pounds of currants; and mix them all well with the meat. Season with a spoonful of powdered cinnamon, a powdered nutmeg, a little mace, and a few cloves, pounded, and one pound of brown sugar; add a quart of Madeira wine and half a pound of citron cut into small bits. This mixture put down in a stone jar and closely covered will keep several weeks. It makes a rich pie for Thanksgiving and Christmas.

Raspberry Jam.

Weigh equal proportions of pounded loaf (or lump) sugar and raspberries; put the fruit in a preserving pan, and with a silver spoon or flat wooden stick bruise and mash it well. Let it boil up; then add the sugar, stirring it well with the fruit; when it boils skim it, and then boil fifteen or twenty minutes.

Strawberry Jam.

Made in the same manner as raspberry jam.

Peach Jam.

Gather the peaches when quite ripe, peel and stone them, put them into a preserving pan, and make them over the fire till hot; rub them through a seive, and add to a pound of pulp the same weight of powdered loaf sugar, and half an ounce of bitter almonds, blanched and pounded; let it boil ten or twelve minutes; stir and skim it well.

To Preserve Damsons.

To every pound of damsons allow three-quarters of a pound of powdered sugar; put into jars or well-glazed earthen pots, alternately a layer of damson and one of sugar; tie strong paper or cloth over the pots, and set them in the oven after the bread is drawn; and let them stand till the oven is cold. The next day, strain off the syrup and boil it till thick; when it is cold, put the damsons into small jars or glasses, pour over the syrup which should cover them, and tie a wet bladder or strong cloth over them.

Melted Butter.

Always use sweet butter; if in the least injured, it spoils the gravy. To make it of the best quality, cut two ounces of butter into little bits, put these in a clean stew-pan, with a large tea-spoonful of flour and a table-spoonful of milk.

When thoroughly melted and mixed, add six table-spoonsful of water, hold it over the fire, and shake it round every minute (all the time one way) till it just begins to simmer; then let it stand quietly and boil up. It should be of the thickness of good cream.

Parsely and Butter

Is made by adding parsely that has been boiled a few minutes and chopped fine to the melted butter.

Egg Sauce

Is made by putting two or three hard boiled eggs, minced fine, into melted butter. The butter need not be as thick when eggs are to be added.

White Sauce for Boiled Fowl.

Melt in a tea-cupful of milk a large table-spoonful of butter kneaded in a little flour; beat up the yolk of an egg with a tea-spoonful of cream, stir it into the butter, and put it over the fire, stirring it constantly: chopped parsley may be added.

Caper Sauce

Is made by adding one or two spoonsful of capers to melted butter.

Oyster Sauce.

Beard and scald the oysters, strain the liquor, and thicken it with a little flour and butter, squeeze in a little lemon-juice, and add three table-spoonsful of cream. Heat it well, but do not let it boil.

Bread Sauce.

Boil half a pint of milk, and put into it a tea-cupful of bread crumbs a little powdered, a small chopped onion which has been boiled in three waters, and let it simmer twenty minutes; then add a piece of butter as arge as a walnut: boil up and serve.

Tomato Sauce.

Peel and slice twelve tomatoes, and pick out the seeds; add three pounded crackers, and pepper and salt to your taste: stew twenty minutes.

Tomato Catsup.

Take two quarts skinned tomatoes, two table-spoonsful of salt, the same of black pepper, and one of allspice; four pods of red pepper, two table-spoonsful of ground mustard; mix and rub these thoroughly together, and stew them slowly, in a pint of vinegar, for three hours; then strain the liquor through a seive, and simmer it down to one quart of catsup. Put this in bottles and cork it tight.

Plum Cake.

Make a cake of two cups of butter; two cups of molasses; two eggs; one cup of milk or buttermilk; one tea-spoonful of salæratus, or volatile salts (which is better); a *gill* of brandy; one tea-spoonful of essence of lemon; and flour to make it a stiff batter.

Beat it well; then add one pound of raisins stoned and chopped; one pound of currants, well washed and dried by the fire; and one or two quarters of citron. Bake in a quick oven. This is a fine rich cake easily made, and not expensive.

Cream Cup Cake.

Four cups of flour; two cups of sugar; three cups of cream; and four eggs. Beat it well, and in square tin pans. When cold, cut it in squares. Bake in a quick oven.

Sandwiches.

These are made of different articles, but always in the same manner.

Cold buscuit sliced thin, and buttered, and a very thin slice of boiled ham, tongue, or beef, between each two slices of biscuit, is best.

Home-made bread cuts better for sandwiches than baker's bread. The meat in sandwiches is generally spread with mustard; the most delectable are those made with boiled smoked tongue.

To Make Coffee.

Take a table-spoonful of fresh-browned and ground coffee for each person (or a pint of water); break white of eggs into it enough to moisten it; stir it well together; then put it in the coffee-kettle and pour boiling water into it; then cover it close, and set it where it will simmer, but not boil, for an hour; it will then be clear, and have the color of brandy. Coffee may be made in this way the day before it is wanted. Pour it off clear, and when wanted, heat it in a coffee-pot. A little isinglass clarified, and used in the place of egg, is equally good, if not an improvement. Loaf sugar and boiled milk to be served with it, allowing each person to suit their own taste. The yolks of eggs beaten and stirred into the boiling milk enrich it. Some persons like the flavor of vanilla in coffee; if so, boil a vanilla bean in the milk.

Chicken Salad.

Mince the white meat of a chicken fine, or pull it in bits. Chop the white parts of celery; prepare a salad dressing thus: Rub the yolks of hard boiled eggs smooth with a spoon: put to each yolk one tea-spoonful of made mustard, half as much salt, a table-spoonful of oil, and a wine-glass of strong vinegar; put the celery in a glass salad bowl; lay the chicken on that; then pour it over the dressing. Lettuce cut small in the place of celery may be used; cut the whites of the eggs in rings to garnish the salad.

Christmas Plumb Pudding.

Chop half a pound of beef suet very fine, stone and chop one pound of raisins; wash, pick clean from grit, and dry, a pound of currants; soak half of a sixpenny loaf of bread in a pint of milk; when it has taken up all the milk, add to it the raisins, currants, chopped suet, and two eggs beaten, a table-spoonful of sugar, one wine-glass of brandy, one nutmeg grated, and any other spice that may be liked. Boil four hours. For sauce, beat a quarter of a pound of butter to a cream, then stir into it half a pound of powdered loaf sugar. Or, melt butter and sugar, and if liked, add more brandy.

Plum Pudding.

Take half a pound of flour, half a pound of raisins stoned and chopped, and some currants washed, picked and dried; use milk enough to stir easily with a spoon; add half a pound of suet chopped fine, a tea-spoonful of salt, and four well beaten eggs; tie it in a floured cloth, and boil four hours. The water must boil when it is put in, and continue boiling until it is done.

Mutton Broth.

Take a neck of mutton, cut it in pieces, reserving a good sized piece to serve in the tureen; put it into cold water enough to cover it, and cover the pot close; set it on coals until the water is lukewarm, then pour it off, and skim it well; then put it again to the meat with the addition of five pints of water, a tea-spoonful

of rice or pearl-barley, and an onion cut up set it on
a slow fire, and when you have taken all the scum off,
put in two or three quartered turnips. Let it simmer
very slowly for two hours, then strain it through a
sieve into the tureen ; add pepper and salt to taste.

Lobster Soup.

After having boiled the lobster, take it from the shell,
roll two or three crackers, and put it to the meat,
which may be cut small; melt some butter in a stew-
pan, two quarts of boiling milk or water, and salt and
pepper to taste : let it boil for half an hour ; put some
crackers in a tureen ; pour over the soup, and serve.

Oyster Mouth Soup.

Make a rich mutton broth, and pour it on the oysters ; add a good bit of butter rolled in flour, and let
it simmer gently for fifteen minutes, then pour it over
some whole crackers and serve.

Savoy Soup.

Cut into quarters and boil in clear water, one or two
heads of savoy cabbage ; when tender drain the water
off, and press all the water from them ; then put them
to as much beef-broth as will cover them ; put it into
a closely covered stew-pan over a moderate fire for
two hours ; then set on the fire a large frying-pan with
a quarter of a pound of fresh butter ; shake some flour
from a dredging-box into it, and let it brown ; stir all
the time ; peel and cut up two onions, and stir them
well about ; as soon as they are nicely colored, add it
to the soup ; soak some rolls or crackers in a quart of
boiling milk or water, and add it to the soup. Mutton
or veal broth may be used.

Cabbage Soup.

Boil corned beef in a pot of water until half done,
then add two small heads of cabbage, cut in quarters,
and well washed (examine carefully, as insects are
sometimes concealed between the leaves) ; when it is
done tender, take out the largest pieces and drain them
in a colander, and set it over a pot of hot water to
keep it hot; if the meat is tender, take that up also,

and add to the soup a cup of pearl-barley or rice, a dozen or more potatoes peeled and cut in half; two or three turnips and some sliced or grated carrots—if liked, an onion or two may also be added; let it boil until the vegetables are all done; put the meat on a large dish, and the cabbage and other vegetables on small dishes, for side dishes. This makes a good family dinner. Serve the soup in a tureen, hot; thicken with a table-spoonful of flour made in thin paste with water.

Turtle Soup.

Cut the head of the turtle off the day before you dress it, and place the body so as to drain it well from blood; the next day cut it up in the following manner: Divide the back, belly, fins, and head from the intestines and lean parts; take care to cut the gall clean out without breaking; scaled in boiling water the first named parts, so as to take off the skin and shell; cut them in pieces small enough to stew, and throw them into cold water; boil the back and belly in water long enough to extract the bones; put the meat on a dish, then make a good stock of a leg of veal, lean ham and the flesh of the inside of the turtle; draw it down to a color, then fill it up with beef stock, and the liquor and bones of the boiled turtle. Season with stalks of marjoram, and boil some onions, a bunch of parsley, cloves and whole pepper. Let it boil slowly for four hours, then strain it to the pieces of back, fins. belly, and head of the turtle; take the bones from the fins, and cut the rest in neat square pieces with as little waste as possible. Thicken the stock with butter rolled in flour, and boil it, to cleanse it from grease and scum; then strain it through a cloth—then boil your herbs that have been washed and pickled, in a bottle of Madeira wine with a little sugar. The herbs to be used are marjoram, thyme, basil, and parsley; then put together soup, herbs, meat. and some forcemeat, and egg-bails. Boil it for a short time, and put it away in clean pans until the following day, as the rawness will go off, and the flavor be improved by so doing. In cutting up the turtle the fat should be taken great care of. It should be separated, cut in neat pieces, and stewed tender in a little of the soup, and put into the tureen at last.

Chicken Soup.

An old fowl makes good soup. Cut it up—first take off the wings, legs, and neck, then divide it down the sides, and cut the back and breast each in two pieces; cut half a pound of pork in thin slices, and put it with the cut up fowl into four or five pints of water; set it over a gentle fire, skim it clear, taking care not to keep it open longer than is necessary; add a cup of rice or pearl-barley, cayenne and black pepper to taste, a leek sliced, and potatoes cut in half—if liked, a grated or sliced carrot, and a turnip cut small may be added.

Another Chicken Soup.

Take two or thrree pounds of veal or vegetables and one small chicken cut up; boil these in two quarts of water; cut up four onions or a leek; grate two carrots and add them to the soup; salt and peper to taste—skim it clear. Other vegetables may be substituted or added as may be preferred; thicken the soup with a little batter or flour and water, with an egg beaten in.

Stock for Gravy Soup or Gravy.

Cut a knuckle of veal into slices, and a pound of lean beef; put these with the knuckle bone into two quarts of water; cover it close and let it stew till very tender. When made in this way, it may be used for soups or gravies.

Mock Turtle Soup.

Take one pound and a half of lean veal, or tripe (which is best), cut it in small slices, and fry of a delicate brown. Cut the meat from three cow-heels in tolerably large pieces, then put it with the fried veil or tripe into a pint and a half of week gravy, with three anchovies, a little salt, some cayenne pepper, three blades of mace, nine cloves, the green parts of three leeks, three sprigs of lemon thyme, some parsley and lemon peel; chop these last very fine before adding them; let the whole stew gently for three hours —then squeeze the juice of three lemons to it; add three glasses of Madeira wine, and let it stew for one hour more,—then skim off the fat and serve.

Salmon.

When salmon is fresh and good, the gills and flesh are of a bright red, the scales clear, and the fish is stiff. When just killed, there is a whiteness between the flakes, which by keeping, melts down, and the fish becomes richer.

Salmon requires to be well boiled, as it is very unwholesome when under-done; boil with horse-radish in the water, anchovy, lobster, or plain drawn butter-sauce; garnish with horse-radish, and sliced lemon

Boiled Salmon.

Run a packthread through the tail, centre of the body, and head of fish, to bring it in the form of a letter S—then put it into a kettle with spring water, and plenty of salt. Cut three or four slanting gashes on each side of the fish, before making it in a form, otherwise skin will break and disfigure the fish; serve with lobster-sauce.

Broiled Salmon.

Cut some slices (about an inch thick); season with pepper and salt; wrap each slice in half a sheet of well buttered white paper; twist the ends of the paper and broil them over a fire of bright coals for ten minutes: serve in the butter with drawn butter or anchovy sauce.

Dried Salmon.

Cut the fish down the back, take out the inside and roe; scale it, and rub the whole with common salt, and hang it to drain for twenty-four hours. Pound three or four ounces of saltpetre, two ounces of coarse salt, and two ounces of brown sugar; mix these well, and rub into the salmon, and lay it on a large dish for two days; then rub it well with common salt, and in twenty-four hours more it will be fit to dry; wipe it well after draining. Stretch it open with two sticks, and hang it in a wood chimney, or in a dry place.

Broiled Salmon.

Dried salmon is eaten broiled in paper, and only just warmed through. Egg sauce and mashed potatoes are usually served with it; or it may be boiled —or lay it in soak in pure water for an hour or two before boiling; rub the gridiron over a bit of suet; lay on the salmon; shake a little pepper over, and serve.

Broiled Cod.

Split a small cod from head to tail; cut the sides in pieces of about three inches width; dip them in flour, and broil; have some butter, pepper and salt, on a hot dish; lay the fish on this and serve.

Or take the steaks, broil them in the same way, or with buttered paper folded around them.

Fried Cod.

Take steaks of about an inch thickness, dredge them with flour, and fry them in hot fat; or if a small one, cut 't the same as for boiling, and flour it, or first dip it in the beaten yolks of eggs, and then in bread crumbs.

Salt Codfish.

Put the dish in soak over night; tie it in a cloth, and boil in clear water; serve with plain boiled potatoes and drawn butter or egg sauce.

Dried Codfish.

This should always be laid in soak with plenty of water, at least one night before cooking after which scrape it well, and put it in plenty of cold water; let it boil gently; skim it; when done, serve with egg sauce over, or cut hard boiled eggs in slices, lay them over the fish, and serve with drawn butter in a boat.

Stewed Salt Cod.

Scald some cod, scrape it white, then pick it in pieces, and put it in a stew-pan with some butter rolled in flour; milk enough to moisten it, and pepper to taste, and let it stew slowly for some minutes, then serve hot.

To Make a Dish of Cold Boiled Cod.

Take some boiled fish, chop it fine, pour some drawn butter or egg sauce over, add pepper to taste; warm it thoroughly, stirring it to prevent its burning; make a roll, or any other form of it; put little spots of pepper over, and if you please, brown the outside before a fire.

Haddocks.

These are chosen by the same rules, and dressed in the same manner as cod.

A Little Dish of Dried Cod.

Pick some dried cod in flakes, pour boiling water over, scald it once, then throw the water off; put some hot milk or water over, to which add a bit of butter; pepper to taste, and serve.

Codfish Cakes.

First boil the fish, then take the white part, chop it fine, with a chopping-knife, add mashed potatoes, an equal quantity, and form them in cakes, with a raw egg or two, and a little flour; dredge the outside with flour, and fry in hot lard or drippings; garnish with fried parsley.

Shad.

These are chosen by the same rules as other fish; they may be baked, fried or broiled.

Fried Shad.

Scale the fish, cut off the head, and then cut down the back, and take out the entrails: keep the roes to be dressed with the fish, then cut it in two, and cut each side in pieces, about three inches wide; flour them, and fry in hot lard, in which put salt to taste. When the inside (which must always be first cooked in any fish) is done a fine brown, turn the other. The soft roe is much liked by some; fry it in the same manner; as also the eggs from the female shad; these last must be well done.

Salt Mackerel.

Lay them in soak in plenty of clear water before using them at least twelve hours, and fry, or broil them—or put them in a frying-pan. Cover with boiling water, and give them fifteen minutes cooking, then pour off the water; pepper to taste, and serve.

Fresh Mackerel Soused.

After having thoroughly cleaned them, boil them in salt and water until tender; then take them out, lay them in a deep dish; take off the water in which they were boiled, half as much as will cover them; add to it as much more vinegar, some whole pepper, cloves, and a blade or two of mace. Pour it over hot; in two days it will be fit to eat.

COOKERY FOR THE SICK.

A quick made Broth.—Take a bone or two of a neck or loin of motton, take off the fat and skin, set it on the fire in a small tin saucepan that has a cover, with three quarters of a pint of water, the meat being first beaten and cut in thin bits; put in a bit of thyme and parsley, and if approved, a slice of onion. Let it boil very quick, skim it nicely; take off the cover, if likely to be too weak, else cover it. Half an hour is sufficient for the whole process.

A very nourishing Veal Broth.—Put the knuckle of a leg or shoulder of veal, with very little meat to it, an old fowl, and four shank bones of mutton, extremely well soaked and bruised, three blades of mace, ten pepper-corns, an onion, a large bit of bread, and three quarts of water, into a stew-pot that covers close, and simmer in the slowest manner after it has boiled up and been skimmed; or bake it; strain and take off the fat; salt as wanted. It will require four hours.

Broth of Beef, Mutton and Veal.—Put two pounds of lean beef, one pound of scrag of veal, one pound of scrag of mutton, three ounces of pearl barley, sweet herbs and ten pepper-corns, into a nice tin saucepan, with seven quarts of water; to simmer to three or four quarts, and clear from the fat when cold. Add one onion if approved, or the white part of leeks. Soup and broth, made of different meats, are more supporting, as well as better flavored. To remove the fat, take it off when cold, as clean as possible; and if there be still any remaining, lay a bit of clean blotting or cap paper on the broth when in the basin, and it will take up every particle

Calves' Feet Broth.—Boil two feet in three quarts of water to half; strain and set it by; when to be used, take off the fat, put a large teacupful of the jelly into a saucepan with half a glass of sweet wine, a little sugar and nutmeg, and heat it till it be ready to boil, then take a little of it and beat by degrees to the yolk of an egg, and adding a bit of butter the size of a nutmeg, stir it all together, but don't let it boil; grate a bit of fresh lemon peel into it.

Chicken Broth.—Put the body and legs of the fowl, after taking off the skin and rump, into the water it was boiled in, with one blade of mace, one slice of onion, and ten white peppercorns. Simmer till the broth be of a pleasant flavor: if not water enough, add a little. Beat a quarter of an ounce of sweet almonds with a tea-spoonful of water fine, boil it in the broth; strain; and when cool, remove the fat.

Beef Tea.—Cut a pound of fleshy beef in thin slices; simmer with a quart of water twenty minutes, after it has once boiled and been skimmed; season, if approved, with a small portion of salt.

Arrow-Root Jelly—If genuine, is very nourishing, especially for weak bowels. Put into a saucepan half a pint of water, a glass of sherry, or a spoonful of brandy, grated nutmeg and fine sugar; boil once up, then mix it by degrees into a desert-spoonful of arrow-root, previously rubbed smooth with two spoonsful of cold water; then return the whole into the saucepan; stir and boil it three minutes.

Tapioca Jelly.—Choose the largest sort, pour cold water on to wash it two or three times, then soak it in fresh water five or six hours, and simmer it in the same until it becomes quite clear; then add lemon-juice, wine and sugar. The peel should have been boiled in it. It thickens very much.

ETIQUETTE FOR LADIES AND GENTLEMEN.

The Person.

Cleanliness, absolute purity of person, is the first requisite in the appearance of a gentleman or lady. Not only should the face and hands be kept clean, but the whole skin should be subjected to frequent ablutions. Better wear coarse clothes with a clean skin, than silk stockings drawn over dirty feet. Let the whole skin be kept pure and sweet, the teeth and nails and hair, clean; and the last two of medium length, and naturally cut. Nothing deforms a man more than bad hair-cutting, and unnatural deformity in wearing it. Abstain from all eccentricities. *Take a medium between nature and fashion*, which is perhaps the best rule in regard to dress and appearance that can be given.

Dress.

The importance of dresss can scarcely be overrated, but by comparison. It is with the world the outward sign of both character and condition.

A well bred man may be ever so reduced in his wardrobe —his clothes may be coarse and thread-bare, but he seldom wears a coarse, and never a dirty shirt.

The boots should always be clean, and invariably well blacked and polished.

Make a point of buying a good hat. One proper fur-hat worth four or five dollars, when a year old, looks more respectable, than a silk one bought yesterday.

Be as particular as you like about the cut of your pantaloons. Buy strong cloth that will not be tearing at every turn, and if you consult economy and taste at the same time, let them be either black or very dark grey, when they will answer upon all occasions.

The vest allows of some fancy, but beware of being too fanciful. A black satin is proper for any person or any occasion. Nothing is more elegant than pure white. Some colors may be worn for variety, but beware of every thing glaring, in materials or trimmings.

If you have but one coat, it will be a black dress-coat, as there are occasions where no other will answer. Frockcoats are worn in the morning, riding or walking, but never at evening visits, at weddings, or parties. Overcoats are worn for comfort; they need not be fine, and should not be fanciful. Most gentlemen wear a simple, plain, black silk cravat, neatly tied in a bow-knot before. Parties require white or light-kid gloves. Black, or very dark ones, of kid, silk, or linen, are worn, upon all other occasions, except in driving, when buff leather-gloves are preferable.

The best dressed men wear the least jewelry. Of all things avoid showy chains, large rings, and gewgaw pins and broaches. All these things should be left to negroes, Indians, and South Sea islanders.

The most proper pocket-handkerchiefs are of white linen. If figured, or embroidered, they should be very delicately done.

Gloves are worn in the street, at church, and places of amusement. It is not enough to carry them—they are to be worn.

LADIES are allowed to consult fancy, variety, and ornament, more than men, yet nearly the same rules apply. It is the mark of a lady to be always well shod. If your feet are small, don't spoil them by pinching—if large, squeezing them makes them worse.

As you regard health, comfort, and beauty, do not lace too tightly. A waist too small for the natural proportion of the figure, is the worst possible deformity, and produces many others. No woman who laces tight can have good shoulders, a straight spine, good lungs, sweet breath, or is fit to be a wife and mother.

The most elegant dresses are black or white. Common modesty will prevent indecent exposure of the shoulders and bosom. A vulgar girl wears bright and glaring colors, fantastically made; a large, flaring, red, yellow, or sky-blue hat, covered with a rainbow of ribbons, and all the rings and trinkets she can load upon her. Of course, a modest well-bred young lady chooses the reverse of all this. In any assemblage, the most plainly dressed woman is sure to be the most lady-like and attractive. Neatness is better than richness, and plainness better than display. Single ladies dress less in fashionable society than married ones, and all more plainly and substantially for walking or travelling, than on other occasions.

In my opinion, nothing beyond a simple, natural flower, ever adds to the beauty of a lady's head-dress.

It is a general rule applicable to both sexes, that persons

are the best dressed, when you cannot remember how they were dressed. Avoid every thing out of the way, uncommon or grotesque.

Behavior in the Street.

When you meet a gentleman with whom you are acquainted, you bow, raising your hat slightly, with your left hand, which leaves your hand at liberty to shake hands if you stop. If the gentleman is ungloved, you must take off yours, not otherwise.

Meeting a lady, the *rule* is that she should make the first salute, or at least, indicate by her manner, that she recognizes you. Your bow must be lower, and your hat carried further from your head; but you never offer to shake hands; that is *her* privilege.

The right, being the post of honor, is given to superiors and ladies, except in the street, when they take the wall, as farthest from the danger from passing carriages, in walking with or meeting them.

In walking with a lady you are not bound to recognize gentlemen with whom she is not acquainted, nor have they in such cases, any right to salute, much less to speak to you.

Should her shoe become unlaced, or her dress in any manner disordered, fail not to apprise her of it respectfully, and offer your assistance. A gentleman may hook a dress, or lace a shoe, with perfect propriety, and should be able to do so gracefully.

Whether with a lady or gentleman, a street talk should be a short one; and in either case, when you have passed the customary compliments, if you wish to continue the conversation you must say, "Permit me to accompany you."

Don't sing, hum, whistle, or talk to yourself in walking. Endeavor, besides being well-dressed, to have a calm, good natural countenance. A scowl always begets wrinkles. It is best not to smoke at all in public, but none but a ruffian will inflict upon society the odor of a bad cigar, or that of any kind, on ladies.

LADIES are not allowed upon ordinary occasions to take the arm of any one but a relative, or an accepted lover, in the street, and in the day time; in the evening—in the fields, or in a crowd, wherever she may need protection, she should not refuse it. She should pass her hand over the gentleman's arm, merely, but should not walk at arm's length apart, as country girls sometimes do. In walking with a gentleman, the step of the lady must be lengthened, and his shortened, to prevent the hobbling appearance of not keeping step. Of course, the conversation of a stranger, beyond asking a necessary question, must be considered as a gross insult, and repelled with proper spirit.

Visiting.

Of course, you ring or knock, and await the opening of the door. When this is done, you ask for the mistress of the house, not the master.

Should she not be at home or engaged, you leave your card, where cards are used, or your compliments. Where there are several ladies in the family, you may ask for *the ladies*. Where people dine early, calls are not made until some time after dinner—in cities they are made from eleven till three.

You leave over-coat, cane, umbrella, &c., and if the call is of any length, your hat in the entry. A graceful bow, a pleasant smile, an easy way of paying the customary compliments, and suiting them to each person, no lesson can teach. In the presence of ladies, you are only silent when listening to them. You never yawn, nor lounge, on your seat, nor interrupt nor contradict, but by insinuation—you never tell unpleasant news, nor make ill-timed observations. Study to please, by a respectful demeanor, and an easy gaity. It is well to know how to enter a room, but it is much better to know when and how to leave it. If you have made a good impression, a long story may wear it off—if a bad one, being tedious only makes it worse. Don't stand hammering and fumbling, and saying, " Well, I guess I must be going." When you are ready, go at once. It is very easy to say, " Miss Susan, your company is so agreeable, that I am staying longer than I intended, but I hope to have the pleasure of seeing you again soon ; I wish you a good morning ;" and, bowing, smiling, shaking hands, if the hand be proffered, you leave the room, if possible without turning your back ; you bow again at the front door, and if any eyes are following you, you still turn and raise your hat in the street.

Introductions.

The rule is, never to introduce one person to another without knowing that it is agreeable to both. Ladies are always to be consulted beforehand. Gentlemen are introduced *to* ladies, not ladies to getlemen.

A common form is, "Mr. Jones, Mr. Smith—Mr. Smith, Mr. Jones." Messrs. Jones and Smith bow, shake hands, express their happiness at being made acquainted with each other.

When more ceremony is required, the introducer says, "Miss Smith, permit me to introduce Mr. Jones to your acquaintance," or, "allow me to present."

Coffee-house, steamboat, and stage-coach acquaintances last only for the time being. You are not obliged to know them afterwards, however familiar for the time.

Behaviour at Dinner.

There is no situation in which one's breeding is more observed, than at the dinner-table; our work would therefore be incomplete without the proper directions as to its etiquette.

If there are ladies, gentlemen, offer their arms, and conduct them to the dining-room, according to their age or the degree of respect to be shown them.

The lady of the house sits at the head of the table, and the gentleman opposite at the foot. The place of honor for gentlemen is on each side of the mistress of the house—for ladies on each side of the master. The company should be so arranged that each lady will have some gentleman at her side to assist her. Of course, it is every gentleman's duty, first of all to see that ladies near him are attended to.

When napkins are provided, they are at once carefully unfolded, and laid on the knees. Observe if grace is to be said, and keep a proper decorum. If soup is served, take a piece of bread in the left hand, and the spoon in the right, and sip *noislessly* from the *side* of the spoon. Do not take two plates of the same kind of soup, and *never* tip up the plate.

When regular courses are served, the next dish is fish. If silver or wide-pronged forks are used, eat with the fork in the right hand—the knife is unnecessary.

Next come the roast and boiled meats. If possible the knife should never be put in the mouth at all, and if at all, let the edge be turned outward. Any thing taken into the mouth not fit to be swallowed, should be quietly removed with the fingers of the left hand, to that side of the plate. The teeth should be picked as little as possible, and never with fork or fingers. Carefully abstain from every act or observation that may cause disgust, such as spitting, blowing the nose, gulping, rinsing the mouth, &c.

When the ladies leave the table, which they do together, at the signal of the mistress of the house, the gentlemen rise and conduct them to the door of the apartment, and then return to the table. This is in formal parties.

If at dinner you are requested to help any one to sauce, do not pour it over the meat or vegetables, but on one side. If you should have to carve and help a joint, do not load a person's plate—it is vulgar: also in serving soup, one ladleful to each plate is sufficient.

Eat PEAS with a desert spoon: and curry also. Tarts and puddings are to be eaten with a *spoon*.

As a general rule, in helping any one at table, never use a knife where you can use a spoon.

Making a noise in chewing, or breathing hard in eating, are both unseemly habits, and ought to be avoided.

Never pare an apple or a pear for a lady, unless she desires you, and then be careful to use your fork to hold it; you may sometimes offer to *divide a very large pear* with or for a person.

At some tables, large colored glasses, partly filled with water, with a bit of lemon, are brought when the cloth is removed. You dip a corner of your napkin in the water, and wipe your mouth, then rinse your fingers and wipe them on your napkin.

The best general rule for a person unacquainted with the usages of society, is to be cautious, pay attention, and do as he sees others do, who ought to know what is proper. Most of our blunders are the result of haste and want of observation.

Conversation.

The object of conversation is to entertain and amuse To be agreeable, you must learn to be a good listener. A man who monopolises a conversation is a *bore*, no matter how great his knowledge.

Never get into a dispute. State your opinions, but do not argue them. Do not contradict, and, above all, never offend by correcting mistakes or inaccuracies of fact or expression.

Never lose temper—never notice a slight—never seem concious of an affront, unless it is of a gross character

You are not required to defend your friends in company,

unless the conversation is addressed to you; but you may correct a statement of fact, if you know it to be wrong.

Never talk at people, by hints, slurs, inuendoes, and such mean devices. If you have any thing to say, out with it. Nothing charms more than candor, when united with good breeding.

Do not call people by their names, in speaking to them. In speaking of your own children, never "Master" and "Miss" them—in speaking to other people of theirs, never neglect to do so.

It is very vulgar to talk in a loud tone, and indulge in hoarse laughs. Be very careful in speaking of subjects upon which you are not acquainted. Much is to be learned by confessing your ignorance—nothing can be by pretending to knowledge which you do not possess.

Never tell long stories. Avoid all common slang phrases, and pet words.

Of all things, don't attempt to be too fine. Use good honest English—and common words for common things.

General Rules of Behavior.

Having dressed yourself, pay no further attention to your clothes. Few things look worse than a continual fussing with your attire.

Never scratch your head, pick your teeth, clean your nails, or worse than all, pick your nose in company; all these things are disgusting. Spit as little as possible, and never upon the floor.

Do not lounge on sofas, nor tip back your chair, nor elevate your feet.

If you are going into the company of ladies, beware of onions, spirits, and tobacco.

If you can sing or play, do so at once when requested, without requiring to be pressed. On the other hand, let your performance be brief, or, if never so good, it will be tiresome. When a lady sits down to the piano forte, some gentleman should attend her, arrange the music stool, and turn over the leaves.

Meeting friends in a public promenade, you salute them the first time in passing, and not every time you meet.

Never tattle—nor repeat in one society any scandal or personal matter you hear in another. Give your own opinion of people if you please, but never repeat that of others.

Meeting an acquaintance among strangers—in the street,

or a coffee-house, never address him by name. It is vulgar and annoying.

Remarks on Habits.

Habits are easily formed, especially such as are bad; and what to-day seems to be a small affair, will soon become fixed and hold you with the strength of a cable. That same cable you will recollect is formed by spinning and twisting one thread at a time; but when once completed, the proudest ship turns her head towards it, and acknowledges her subjection to its power.

Twelve rules for the formation of good habits: Rule 1st. Have a plan laid before-hand for every day. 2. Acquire the habits of untiring industry. 3. Cultivate perseverance. 4. Cultivate the habit of punctuality. 5. Be an early riser. 6. Be in the habit of learning something from every one with whom you meet. 7. Form fixed principles on which to think and act. 8. Be simple and neat in your personal appearance. 9. Acquire the habit of doing every thing well. 10. Make constant efforts to be master of your temper. 11. Cultivate soundness of judgment. 12. Observe a proper treatment of parents, friends and companions.

LADIES' TOILETTE TABLE.

To Prevent Loosening of the Hair.

Immerse the head in cold water, morning and night, dry the hair thoroughly, and then brush the scalp, until a warm glow is produced. In ladies with long hair this plan is objectionable; and a better one is to brush the scalp until redness and a warm glow are produced, then apply to the roots of the hair one or two of the following lotions.

Lotion for Promoting the Growth of the Hair, and Preventing it from Turning Grey.

No. 1.

Vinegar of cantharides, half an ounce.
Eau de Cologne, one ounce.
Rose-water, one ounce.

No. 2.

Eau de Colegne, two ounces.
Tincture of cantharides, half-an-ounce.
Oil of nutmegs, half-a-drachm.
Oil of lavender, ten drops.
Mix.

To Cure Ringworms.

The head should be washed with a profusion of soap, and the hair carefully combed, to remove all loosened hairs and every particle of crust. Then bathe the head with ringworm lotion.

Ringworm Lotion.

Sublimate of mercury, five grains.
Spirits of wine, two ounces.
Tincture of musk, one drachm.
Rose-water, six ounces.
Mix well.

Style of Bonnet.

A person of delicate pale complexion should wear a hat with pink lining. A person of dark complexion should have white lining, with rose trimming. A person with very red or yellow complexion should not wear high colors.

Dress.

Have reference to the complexion. Tight sleeves without trimming are becoming to full forms, of medium height, or below it. A tall person appears graceful with drapery. A short form should not wear much drapery, and not a full skirt.

Flounces.

Flounces appear well upon tall persons, but never upon diminutive ones.

High-neck Dresses.

High-neck dresses are generally becoming, but not upon a very high-shouldered person. If the shoulders are only moderately high, the neck may be covered, and a narrow piece of lace, instead of a collar, put around the throat.

Evening Dresses.

Evening dresses of transparent materials, look well when made high in the neck. Make the dress loose over the chest, and tight over the shoulder blades. Long sashes fastened in front are preferable to belts, unless there is much trimming upon the dress. Narrow lace at the wrist is becoming, and gives a finish to the dress. An extremely small and waspish-looking waist can never be considered handsome. It is exceedingly hurtful to those who attain it by tight-lacing, and doubly ungraceful, since it prevents all graceful movements.

Short Cloaks.

Short cloaks are very becoming to short and clumsily built persons, but to a tall figure the reverse.

CANARY BIRDS.

General Directions.

Keep the cage washed and clean if you wish the birds to be healthy. Fresh lettuce, cabbage and plantain may be given them in July and August, two or three times a day. The seeds of plantain and lettuce are good to be given as food. Keep clean water in pans in the cage for them to wash and bathe in. A piece of cuttle-fish bone or sand ought to be in the cage, to keep them in a healthy condition. A little sponge cake may be given occasionally. Crackers, sweet apples, and worms are good. Never give salt.

How to Distinguish the Male from the Female.

The male may be distinguished from the female by a streak of bright yellow over the eyes and under the throat; his head is wider and longer, and has richer colors, and larger feet. He also begins to warble first, which is often at a month old.

LETTER WRITER.

1. A letter of introduction, note of invitation, or reply, should always be enclosed in an envelope.
2. A letter of introduction should always enclose the card and address of the person introduced.
3. Notes of invitation should always be sent in the name of the lady of the house.
4. Invitations should be answered within two days.
5. Notes of invitation should not be sealed.
6. Figured and colored paper is out of style; pure white paper, with gilt edges, is more strictly in good taste.

THE LADY'S WORK BOX.

PREPARATION OF FRAMES.

To Dress a Frame for Cross Stitch.

The canvass must be hemmed neatly around: then count your threads, and place the centre one exactly in the middle of the frame. The canvass must be drawn as tight as the screws or pegs will permit, and if too long, it should be wrapped around the poles with tissue paper, to keep it from dust, and the friction of the arms, as that is essential to the beauty of the work. It must in all cases be rolled *under*, or it will occasion much trouble in the working. When laced quite even in the frame, secure, by fine twine passed over the stretchers and through the canvass, very closely; both sides must be tightened gradually, or it will draw to one side, and the work will be spoiled.

To Dress a Frame for Cloth Work.

Stretch your cloth in the frame as tight as possible, the right side uppermost.

The canvass on which you intend to work must be of a size to correspond with the pattern, and must be placed exactly in the centre of the cloth to which it is to be secured, as smooth as possible. When the work is finished, the canvass must be cut, and the threads drawn out, first one way and then the other. It is necessary to be especially careful, in working, not to split the threads, as that would prevent them drawing, and would spoil the appearance of the work. In all cases, it is advisable to place the cloth so as that the nap may go downward. In working bouquets of flowers, this rule is indispensable. The patterns for cloth work should be light and open. It looks well for sofas, arm chairs, &c., but is by no means so durable as work done with wool entirely on canvass.

Materials for Working.

Canvass (coarse) eighteen threads to the inch. Work in cross stich with double wool. This is proper for a footstool, sofa-pillow, &c.

Canvass (very coarse) ten threads to the inch. Work in cross stitch, over one thread, with single wool. If used for grounding, work in two threads. This will accelerate the work, and look equally well.

STITCHES.

1. *Tent Stitch.*

This is accomplished over one thread the cross way, and should be done in a frame. In grounding, perform the work the bias way of the canvass, and work from left to right.

2. *Cross Stitch.*

Let the wool be put across two threads, and the needle down two, working the cross way, and finishing as the work progresses.

3. *Straight Cross Stitch.*

This stitch is the same as Cross Stitch, but is worked the straight way of the canvass; and although on coarse canvass, has a very pleasing and finished appearance.

4 *Windsor Stitch.*

Pass the wool over six threads straight, and six threads down, which will prevent a square when the section row is completed.

5. *Pavilion Stitch.*

Four threads having been taken straight down, bring the needle down one thread; after that take two threads, then four, as before, and finish the row. Commence the second row with a stitch in two threads, then take four and so proceed. Gold beads tastefully introduced have a very pretty effect.

6. *Josephine Stitch.*

This is a very pretty stitch for bags with gold or silver braid, and is executed in stripes from the bottom to the top. Take six threads straight, and proceed to the end of the row; after which take three lengths of braid, and work one of them in Cross Stitch, diamond fashion.

7. *Berlin Stitch.*

Work this stitch in a scollop, taking six threads straight down. Much of the beauty of it depends upon the contrast of color (having an eye to harmony) in the threads. The effect should be ascertained before beginning the work.

8. *Czar Stitch.*

We have heard this called *Economic* Stitch. It is worked over from six to eight threads in depth, and two in width, crossed from right to left. Gold thread should be interposed between each row.

9. *Irish Stitch.*

Four, six, or eight threads are to be taken straight, two threads being left between. The second row is to be begun four threads up, between the two threads left on the former row; take care that the stitches meet the first row. This is a valuable stitch, easily worked into a variety of pretty forms.

Perforated Card.

The needles must not be too large, or the holes will be liable to get broken. The smaller ones must be worked in silk; the larger patterns may be done either in silk or wool. Sometimes the flowers are worked in Chenille, and the leaves in silk; this gives to card cases, &c., a beautiful and highly ornamental appearance.

Bead Work.

Use the canvass called bolting; and work two threads each way on the slant, with china silk, taking especial care that the beads are all turned the same way, that the whole may appear uniform. Work the pattern with thick beads and ground with transparent ones. You must, in this kind of work, have as few shades as possible.

Rug Bordering.

When we descend into the arena of domestic utility, it is vastly surprising in how many ways the Art of Needlework adapts itself to comfort and to ornament. We may presume carpets to be too unwieldy for the management of fair fingers; but *rugs* come within the compass of the fair Artist's skill and taste. Many of the borderings completed by English ladies are quite equal to the labored productions of the *Gobelins*: and are of course, at all times superior to those which emenate from the loom.

Gothic Chairs.

For dark-framed chairs choose light patterns; tent stitch being grounded in cross stitch, as may be seen in the private apartments at Windsor Castle. Sometimes a sort of cushion is inserted in the back, and the whole is done in cloth or satin, and the canvass withdrawn. Flower embroidery, gem patterns, and braiding, are all made use of in this description of work.

Settees.

These should be executed in cloth, thirty-three inches long and twenty-six wide.

Sofa Pillows.

Work the squares of canvass with flowers in preference to any other pattern, and finish with damask, trimming with silk cord, tassels, &c.

· There are few subjects on which more taste may be exercised than on these. A certain fulness approaching to largeness is desirable in the design, otherwise the pillow will be lost in the more massive attributes of the sofa itself.

Weight Cushions.

These may be obtained ready-made, and afterwards covered with any variegated pattern of needlework. They are very useful.

Wire Baskets.

These should be of silver ware, and worked in silk.

Slippers

Are worked in embroidery, on canvass, satin, or soft kid.

Fire-Side Caps.

These are worked in gems, or flowers, or velvet. Embroidery and gold braid are also adopted. There are several pieces joined together to fit the head, and the top is a handsome tassel.

DIRECTIONS FOR COLORING GARMENTS, &c.

Discharging Colors.

Colored silks are put into a copper vessel, in which put water, with half a pound of soap dissolved. Then boil until the copper gives evidence of color. Then take out the silk, and rinse it in warm water. Then add more soap, and boil as before, until the color is discharged.

Re-Dying Silks, or Changing the Color.

You can dye all colors, black—blues, green or black—green, brown—and brown, green.

To Dye Silk, Light-Blue.

Boil your silk in a solution of white soap and water until it is white; then rinse in warm water. Put the silk into a wash-basin, and cover it with cold water. From your chemic blue-bottle drop one or two drops: this is sufficient, unless you wish to have the color darker—in which case, more of your chemic blue must be used. Move your silk in the water until the blue is expended, which can be ascertained by holding up some water with your hand, and looking through it as it falls.

To Dye Silks, Green.

A quarter of a pound of ground ebony-wood placed in a dish, and boiling water poured over it, stirred, covered over with a cloth a few moments, and strained off—will color the silk, if put into the mixture for half an hour, grass-green, inclining to laurel. After the half hour, take the silk out, and rinse in the same dish. Pour cold spring water into another dish, and put in a table-spoonful and a quarter of chemic blue; then rinse in spring water, and dry.

PROFESSOR LEIBEG'S
CELEBRATED WASHING RECIPE,

OR CELEBRATED CHEMICAL, GENERALLY KNOWN BY H. TWELVETREE'S OR MADAME BEAVELT'S WASHING RECIPE.

RICHLY WORTH TWENTY DOLLARS,
AS
IT SAVES POUNDING AND RUBBING

☞ *The Recipe, in a separate form, is generally sold at Fifty Cents and One Dollar each.*

MIXTURE.—Dissolve half a pound of Soda in a gallon of Boiling Water, and pour upon it a quarter of a pound of Lime. After this has settled, cut up ten ounces of common bar Soap, and strain the solution upon it, and mix perfectly. Great care must be taken that no particles of Lime are poured upon the Soap. Prepare the Mixture the evening before washing.

DIRECTIONS.—To ten gallons of water add the above Preparation, when the water is boiling; and put the clothes in while boiling. Each lot of linen must boil half an hour, and the same liquid will answer for three batches of clothes. The white clothes must be put in soak over night, and, if the collars and wristbands are soaped and rubbed slightly, so much the better. Clean cold water may be used for rinsing. Some prefer boiling them for a few moments in clean blueing water and afterwards rinse in cold water.

To Dye Silk Brown, Inclining to Mulberry.

Boil, about two hours, two ounces of sumach or one ounce of galls, one ounce of logwood, two or three ounces of camwood or madder. Pour in cold water, and cool it down. If necessary to incline more to mulberry, add a little purple archil. Put in the silk, and simmer it for half an hour or more. Rinse in two waters, and hang up the silk to dry.

To Dye Silks, Red, Crimson, &c.

Dissolve two ounces of white soap in boiling water. Stir your silk shawl or dress in the liquid, rubbing with your hand any places looking soiled, until it is as clean as possible. Put it into one or two more of the same kind. Then rinse in warm water. Put the silk in a solution, in hot water, of half an ounce of Spanish annatto, and stir for half an hour. Take it out, and rinse in clean water. Then put the silk into a solution of alum, (size of a common bean,) in warm water. Take out, and rinse in clear water. Boil in copper, 20 minutes, a quarter of an ounce of cochineal. Dip into a pan. Put silk in for thirty minutes. For scarlet, add to the above half a wine-glassful of the solution of tin. When cold, rinse in cold water.

To Dye Black, Common Materials.

Four pounds of logwood for four pounds of goods. Soak logwood twelve hours in soft water. Boil an hour, and strain. Dissolve one ounce of blue vitriol in warm water, and dip goods into it. Then turn the whole into logwood dye. If they are cotton goods, boil fifteen minutes, stirring, to prevent spotting. Drain, and do not wring goods. Hang them up to dry. Put them into water boiling hot, in which there is half a tea-cupful of salt for two gallons of water. This sets the color. Goods must remain until the water is cold, and then dried without wringing. To set color for black silk, put it into boiling hot suds.

To Clean Silk Goods.

If dingy, rub dry bran on them carefully with a woolen cloth. Hard soap is best for washing silks of all colors except yellow—and soft soap for that. Dissolve soap in hot water, then add cold, to make it lukewarm. Put in silks, and rub until clean. Take them out without ringing, and rinse in two portions of warm water. Add sulphuric acid enough to give it an acid taste, for bright yellows, maroons, and crimsons. To restore pink colors, add a little vinegar to the second rinsing water. For blues, purple, &c., add pearlash. For scarlet, a solution of tin. For olive-green, a little verdigris dissolved in the water. Fawn and brown, in pure water. Fold up silks while damp; after drying awhile, iron them on the wrong side, with irons just hot enough to smooth them.

To Clean Carpets.

Take up and shake at least twice a year, if used much; and once, if not used, to keep out moths. Put straw under, to prevent dust grinding them out. If any moths are found, sprinkle tobacco or ground pepper on floor underneath. To remove grease, grate on clay or chalk very thick; cover it with brown paper, and put on a warm iron. Repeat it until removed. If it needs cleansing all over, spread it on a clean floor, and rub on, with a new broom, pared and grated raw potatoes. Dry perfectly.

To Clean White Kid Gloves.

Rub on India-rubber, moist bread, or magnesia. If you cannot clean in this way, close the top of the gloves, and rub them over with a sponge saturated with saffron-water. The color will be yellow or brown.

To Take out Ink from Floors.

Scour with sand wet with sulphuric acid and water. Then rinse with strong pearl-ash water.

MISCELLANEOUS.

To Make Fine Polish Blacking.

Take of ivory black and molasses each twelve ounces, spermaceti oil four ounces, white wine vinegar four pints, mix all together.

Summer Drink.

Three pounds of sugar, 5 gills of molasses, 2 ounces of tartaric acid, 3 pints of water.

For Cleaning Britannia.

Rub the article all over with a piece of woolen cloth, moistened with sweet oil, then apply a little pounded rotten-stone, or polishing paste, with the finger, till the polish is produced, after which wash it well with soap and hot water, and when dry, wipe off smartly with soft wash leather and a little fine whiting.

To Keep Out Red Ants.

Place in the closet, or wherever they appear, a small quantity of green sage.

Ice Cream

May be made thus: Put milk over a gentle fire to boil, and stir it occasionally; beat four eggs for each quart until very light, then stir them into the boiling milk; stir it for a few minutes, then set it to become cold;

make it very sweet, flavor it to taste, then freeze it
If it is flavored with the juice of berries or pineapple,
bruise the fruit, strain the juice from it, and put it in
the cream when cold.

Pickling.—Cucumbers.

Pick the small, green cucumbers. Turn on boiling
water; and in four or five hours take them out, and
put them in cold vinegar, with a spoonful of alum
and a tea-cupful of salt to every gallon of vinegar.
Turn the vinegar from the cucumbers; scald and
skim it; then turn it on the pickles, and scald them
without boiling, a few minutes. Then put them hot
in the vessel for keeping. To make them brittle,
scald several times. Put in a few peppers.

Oysters.

Turn off the liquor from the oysters; strain and boil
it. Rinse off the bits of shells. Put the oysters in the
liquor while boiling, and boil one minute. Take them
out, and put in the liquor a few pepper-corns, cloves,
and a blade or two of mace. Add a little salt, and as
much vinegar as oyster sauce. Boil the whole fifteen
minutes, and turn it on the oysters. Bottle and
cork them, if you wish to keep them several weeks.

Preserving Apples.

Take equal weights of good brown sugar and of
apples; peel or wash, core, and chop the apples fine,
allow to every three pounds of sugar a pint of water;
dissolve, then boil the sugar pretty thick, skimming
it well; add the apples, the grated peel of one or
two lemons, and two or three pieces of white ginger,
and boil till the apples look clear and yellow. This
will keep for years. Crab-apples done in this way,
without paring, are next to cranberries.

www.ingramcontent.com/pod-product-compliance
Lightning Source LLC
Chambersburg PA
CBHW022133160426
43197CB00009B/1263